Longhi's

Longhi's

Recipes and Reflections from Maui's Most Opinionated Restauranteur

Bob Longhi
and
Gabrielle Longhi

Photography by Gabrielle Longhi

Ten Speed Press
Berkeley, California

Ten Speed Press
Box 7123
Berkeley, California 94707
www.tenspeed.com

Distributed in Australia by Simon & Schuster Australia, in Canada by Ten Speed Press Canada, in New Zealand by Southern Publishers Group, in South Africa by Real Books, in the United Kingdom and Europe by Airlift Books, and in Singapore, Malaysia, and Indonesia by Berkeley Books.

Special thanks to the following, who kindly loaned art, glassware, flatware, ceramicware, and other props for the photos: The Mercantile (808-572-1407), Makawao, Hawaii; Ola's Makawao, Makawao, Hawaii; Madaline Michaels Gallery, Lahaina, Hawaii; Todd Campbell, Wailuku, Hawaii.

Library of Congress Cataloging-in-Publication Data
Longhi, Bob.
    Longhi's : recipes and reflections from Maui's most opinionated restauranteur / Bob Longhi and Gabrielle Longhi ; photography by Gabrielle Longhi.
              p.   cm.
    Includes index.
    ISBN 0-89815-950-4 (cloth)
    1. Cookery, Italian. 2. Longhi's (Restaurant) I. Longhi, Gabrielle.
II. Title.
TX723.L587 1998
641.5945--dc21   97-45488
                                      CIP

Printed in Hong Kong

First printing, 1997

3 4 5 6 7 8 9 10 — 02 01 00 99

Design by Catherine Jacobes.
Photography and hand-tinting by Gabrielle Longhi, Los Angeles.
Food styling by Carol O'Leary, Lahaina, Hawaii.
Photo styling assistance and props by De Borah Hoopingarner, Lahaina, Hawaii.

Photo credits:
Page 26 (Spaghetti Putana): tablecloth by Palais Royal and flatware by Sabre France from The Mercantile. Page 36 (Manicotti): tea towel by Palais Royal from The Mercantile. Page 42 (Mussels Marinara): tea towel by Palais Royal and shell bowl by Bopla from The Mercantile. Page 44 (Lobster Longhi): linens by Palais Royal and flatware by Sabre France from The Mercantile. Page 51 (Fruitti di Mare): tea towel by Palais Royal from The Mercantile. Sea shells from Madaline Michaels Gallery. Page 60 (Ahi Torino): flatware by Scoff France from The Mercantile. Page 70 (Chicken Mediterranean): flatware by Sabre France from The Mercantile. Page 84 (Artichoke Longhi): tea towel by Palais Royal, artichoke dish and plate by Bopla, and flatware by Sabre France from The Mercantile. Page 88 (Asparagus Parmesan): tea towel by Le Jaquard Francais from The Mercantile. Page 91 (Zucchini Frittata): plate by Aletha Soule and napkin by Palais Royal from The Mercantile. Page 92 (Longhi Salad): Norfolk pine bowl by Todd Campbell. Page 100 (Ahi Carpaccio): tiki glasses by Magic Sands and ceramic leaf platter by Rift Zone from Ola's Makawao. Page 102 (Potato-Crusted Crabcakes): plate by Bopla and linens by Palais Royal from The Mercantile. Page 109 (Grilled Wild Mushrooms): orange napkin by Palais Royal from The Mercantile. Page 115 (Mint Pesto): tablecloth by Palais Royal from The Mercantile. Page 122 (Grilled Lamb Chops): tablecloth by Palais Royal from The Mercantile. Page 129 (Amaretto-Lemon Cheesecake): tablecloth by Palais Royal from The Mercantile. Page 133 (Chocolate-Dipped Macaroons and Strawberries): napkin by Palais Royal from The Mercantile. Page 147 (Coconut Haupia Cream Pie): tablecloth by Palais Royal from The Mercantile. Page 151 (Chocolate-Raspberry Truffle Cake): Cordials by Union Street Glass from Ola's Makawao.

For more information about Longhi's, visit their website:
www.longhi-maui.com

To the Longhi family and the many employees, past and present,
who have made Longhi's so wonderful.

FIRST, WE WISH TO THANK Carol O'Leary for finding the time to test all of the recipes while running the kitchen of an extremely busy restaurant and for preparing the beautiful food for the photography when it had to be done during the busiest time of the year. This book could not have been completed without her.

We also thank Randy Ortega, for his recipes and beautiful baking; Sally Longhi, for her wonderful enthusiasm, great taste, and kind support; Michael Robinson, for his encouragement and ideas; DeBorah Hoopingarner, for her excellent assistance with the photography and her tireless dedication to the project; Eddy McCafferty, for his behind-the-scenes help and always positive attitude; and Mark O'Leary, Melchor Jacinto, and Guy Corti, for their reliable help in the kitchen.

Many thanks to Stephanie Kest and Elaine Freedman of The Mercantile, as well as to Shari O'Brian and Cindy Heacock of Ola's Makawao, for generously allowing us to borrow linens, flatware, glassware, ceramics, and other props from their beautiful stores for the photography; to Todd and Cindy Abrams of the Madaline Michaels Gallery; to Trav Duro of MISTER WINE; and to Sally, Peter, and Perrie Longhi, Todd Campbell, and Ann Casey, who loaned us ceramics, glassware, and numerous other props.

To Phil Wood, Jo Ann Deck, Lorena Jones, Catherine Jacobes, and all at Ten Speed Press who contributed to the book, thank you.

Special thanks to Randi Humm Masotti for her invaluable contributions to the creation of Longhi's, and for being with us through our critical opening years.

And lastly, thanks to Peter Longhi for quietly running Longhi's and keeping things humming along for the past eighteen years.

Contents

LONGHI'S RESTAURANT celebrated its twentieth anniversary on December 26, 1996. For years many of my customers have been asking me when I was going to write a cookbook. My standard answer was, "The time will come." Well, the time has come. My daughter Gabrielle, a writer and well-known artist, suggested that she and I join forces and finally write about the food of Longhi's. This book, the result of our collaboration, is not a cookbook in the standard sense, but a book about food and philosophy that happens to have most of the recipes that have made Longhi's restaurant so successful.

In viewing cooking shows and reading many of the newer cookbooks, I've noticed that the current trend is to make everything complicated. The older cookbooks I have been reading for several years have recipes that were never so intricate, never so long, and that never used ingredients so difficult to procure. It seems to me that the experts want everyone to think that cooking is a recondite endeavor that can only be understood by a few people. I've entitled these ventures "gastronomic rococo."

After the architecture and art of the Renaissance, the Baroque period emerged, followed by the rococo style of the eighteenth century, each period becoming more ornate. Eventually these art forms evolved into the present style, which is the opposite of rococo and is very utilitarian.

In this book we are the opposite of rococo. We want to show everyone—as I do on my cooking show—that anyone can be a great cook. All you have to do is put your attention where it belongs. These recipes use ingredients that are not difficult to find. They are not complicated, and do not require a multitude of procedures in order to accomplish the result. They can be cooked quickly, and if you follow the instructions, you will get results that will make you very happy. This book is more about food, ingredients, and imagination than it is about technique.

When I lived in New York City and Washington, D.C., and traveled throughout the world, I thought it was very difficult to get a great meal unless you played the game of the restauranteurs. Gael Greene, one of the most respected New York food critics, wrote a book whose theme was the masochistic attitude of New York diners. It had become de rigueur in New York to be treated badly when you went into a restaurant. The waiters were insouciant, the owners were impolite, and basically the attitude of the people working in the restaurants toward the customers was not one of good will. Fortunately the food was usually excellent and the service adequate even though the waiters were often indifferent. The total experience was lacking because cheerfulness, friendliness, and good will are necessary components of a great dining experience.

When I opened Longhi's, I wanted to create an establishment that had all the elements of my favorite restaurants: great food, great service, and wonderful atmosphere. I wanted to have a place where diners could dress the way they wanted to dress and did not have to conform to the wishes of the restaurants' owners. I remember going to New

York City in June one year when the temperature was almost 100 degrees. Even though I had lived in Hawaii for several years, I had never been so hot. The restaurant at which we dined had inadequate air-conditioning, but the owner insisted that every man wear a coat and tie. This to me was an abomination. I told myself at that moment, if I ever open a restaurant, I'll never make my customers uncomfortable just to satisfy rules that I have arbitrarily created.

At Longhi's we have a saying: "You can dress any way you want, and we will treat you as if you are wearing a tuxedo." I feel that you should be able to come to a restaurant dressed the way you want to dress, whether you wear shorts or black tie. I insist that my staff treat our customers with complete respect regardless of their attire.

When you read this book, get comfortable, sit back, and relax. Hopefully, you will enjoy the narratives and, above all, try the recipes. They are not difficult and, who knows, they might inspire you to pursue a dream like the one I had twenty years ago.

The Story of Longhi's

The Making
of a Restauranteur

I GREW UP IN UPSTATE New York in a French/Italian family. My grandmother, Marie, was from Alsace-Lorraine, while my grandfather, Luigi, was from the Como district near Lago Maggiore, seven miles from the famous shoe-manufacturing city of Varise in northern Italy. This area produces more chefs than any place in the world. Grandpa Luigi, who in 1918 was the only Italian in the Connecticut "Who's Who," was not a chef but a master mason and became a builder of large theaters, churches, airports, and roads. Even though Grandpa wasn't a chef, he loved food and was a gigantic eater.

I remember Grandpa stirring the polenta he made for special occasions, to be accompanied by rabbit or wild hare. I was less than ten, so my recollection of whether it was rabbit or wild hare is hazy. I do remember that it was difficult to figure out why everyone thought polenta was so great. It's only cornmeal mush, and my childhood palate was not enthralled. For many years after my grandpa died I never heard the word polenta. We did not eat it at home, and I never saw it served in restaurants. All of a sudden, about ten years ago, somebody in California started raving about polenta. After that, every restaurant in California had polenta with everything *except* wild hare. At Longhi's we rarely serve polenta.

Grandpa Luigi's main contribution to my culinary upbringing was the good fortune he had in meeting and marrying Marie Riche in Great Barrington, Massachusetts, in the late nineteenth century. My grandmother was born a few miles from Nancy, France, the town that is credited as the birthplace of Art Nouveau, and one of the most beautiful cities in the world. That area, like Como, is also noted for its great chefs and culinary talents. Who hasn't heard of Quiche Lorraine?

Thanks to the Germans, whom my grandmother loathed, Marie came to America with her family to avoid the conscription of her brothers into the German army. In 1870 the

Germans occupied Alsace-Lorraine, and the territory has gone back and forth between France and Germany for hundreds of years. The cooking in this area has both French and German overtones, but my Grandma was definitely of the French school. When she met Luigi, he taught her how to cook many northern Italian dishes. She cooked with a unique style, calling her risotto *risuck* and gnocchi *gnock*. Regardless of what she called them, they were the best I ever had. I don't know whether my memory is prejudiced by the old bromide "My Grandmother was the best cook that ever lived," but I thoroughly enjoyed my Grandma's cooking.

My next big influence was their son, my father, Paul Longhi. Paul, half-Italian and half-French, married Eleanor Barrette, one hundred percent French-Canadian. Paul loved food and made sure that our kitchen always had the finest possible ingredients. While Grandma Marie made great risotto, gnocchi, and many of her French specialties, Paul cooked great steaks, lamb chops, and his specialty, Lobster PJ. (Lobster PJ, one of Longhi's best-loved dishes, is described later in the book.)

While at Cornell University (although not enrolled at the famed hotel school), I associated with many "hotelies" and became quite well known for my wine and food parties. Some people might refer to them more as drunken brawls, but in any event we did get to taste many wines during those six-hour events. Prior to my senior year I married Sally, whom I met in the summer of 1952 on the beautiful Lake George beach. As our finances were low, I ventured into my first food business. Every Wednesday I would go to the local Italian bakery and buy one hundred fresh submarine rolls. Sally and I assembled the submarine sandwiches, which I sold at the fraternity houses in two hours. The year was 1956; the subs sold for sixty cents, and my cost (not counting labor) was twenty cents. Even though I was not attending the august Cornell Hotel School, my ability to manage food costs and turn a profit were worthy of an A in class. The profits generated by this business were more than enough to pay our rent each month. After this venture I had a hiatus of twenty years before I would delve back into the food business.

The first Christmas we were married, Sally gave me a copy of *The Gourmet Cookbook*. Up to that point in my life I had cooked very little (except for the submarines), and had mostly enjoyed the labors of other people's skills. This book awakened something inside that inspired the inner chef in me. From that moment on I became a cooking fool. I tried everything, and it all seemed to taste great—at least to me and my friends, who were eating for free … so who knows what their reviews were worth. I, however, for the first time in my life had an image of myself as being a great cook.

The next twenty-year period was extremely important in terms of my development as a future restauranteur. For twenty years I was an insurance agent moonlighting in food philosophy. I lived in New York City and Washington, D.C. My office during my first years in the insurance business was on Park Avenue in the great city of New York. If one wants to experience great restaurants, great food, and great variety, there is not a better place than New York City. I became the food maven of my insurance agency. I not only tried all the famous restaurants but also talked incessantly about these venerable institutions.

During these years my general agent was a bon vivant named Harry Copeland. Harry was a regular at a restaurant that was considered the finest restaurant in New York City: Chambord, owned by the world-famous restauranteur Roger Chauveron. Harry was so forward-thinking that he hired the sous chef from Chambord to cook at our office for prospective clients. I came up with the idea of holding seminars for medical students from the various New York universities at our office with this great chef creating gourmet meals for these hardworking future physicians. It proved to be a fabulous selling tool, and it again showed me that food could also be profitable.

In 1968 Sally and I took our first trip to Europe. During a period of three weeks we dined at the finest restaurants in Italy and ate at ten of the eighteen three-star *Guide Michelin* restaurants in France. This was an extremely exciting time for me, as my culinary IQ was again enhanced by the perfection of these great restaurants. Two of the meals we had in France were particularly memorable. Within one hour of arriving in France I finally tasted the magnificent bouillabaisse prepared in the style only the cooks along the Côte d'Azur are able to produce. The great chef Mère Terrats in La Napoule-Plage personally made me my first bouillabaisse—and it remains the best I've ever eaten. (On my last trip to France I sadly discovered that Mère Terrats had passed away and her restaurant no longer existed.) For many years prior to my trip to Europe I had read that La Pyramide, a restaurant in the small town of Vienne, on the Rhone River seventeen miles south of Lyon, was considered the finest restaurant in the world. The owner, Fernand Point, a gargantuan man who weighed nearly 400 pounds, had created this mecca of gastronomy. Upon his death in 1956 he left the restaurant in the hands of his very capable wife, Mado. The reports were that La Pyramide, sometimes referred to as Chez Point, was still as great as ever under Mado's direction. We arrived with an introduction from Monsieur Raymond Thuilier, the chef-proprietor of another three-star restaurant, Oustau de Baumanière in Les Baux de Provence, where we had spent the last two days luxuriating in that fabulous auberge in southern France. After reading the note from Monsieur Thuilier, Madame Point smiled widely, chatted with us for several minutes, and gave us the best table in the house. We had an unbelievable meal and the best wine experience of my life. The 86-year-old sommelier with a twinkle in his eye recommended an old Côte-Rôtie and a local white wine called Chateau Grillet. I later discovered that Chateau Grillet is considered by most oenophiles as perhaps the finest white wine produced in France. Le Pyramide procures fifty percent of the wine

produced by this vineyard each year. (When I went to the great Parisian restaurant Taillevent in 1985, Monsieur Jean Claude Vrinat, who is one of the great hosts of the restaurant world, told me that his favorite white wine is Chateau Grillet.) I arrived home from Europe twenty pounds overweight, and it took me two months to recover from this eating adventure.

In 1971 I was living in Washington, D.C., eating my way through the town and starting to think about what would someday become Longhi's Cafe. Sally and I had divorced, and I was living with Randi Humm, who was an excellent baker as well as a terrific cook. We lived in a big apartment house that I owned, and we were constantly cooking large meals for friends and family. The tenants looked forward to sampling what we had prepared as our apartment became an unofficial restaurant.

By this time my four children had become old enough to participate in my culinary adventures (though they might call it their enslavement in my kitchen). One of our major family enterprises was the annual Christmas party where I entertained the employees of my insurance agency. Under my instructions Gabrielle, Carol, Peter, and Charlie did all the work needed to prepare the meals. They rarely complained and went at it with willing gusto. Each would have a task: One would cut the melons that we used for prosciutto and melon. (I still believe the finest melons are the ones from Spain that are available in November and December.) Another would chop mushroom stems and add the ingredients for stuffed mushrooms. Another would make a cold beef and cannellini bean salad that I had learned from the famous New York restauranteur Romeo Salta. Another would assemble the lasagne, and Randi would make luxurious desserts. This two-day ordeal always resulted in a great party. I remember sitting around the day after these events and thinking that if we had sold that meal, we would have made a two thousand dollar profit, another spark in my psyche toward Longhi's.

Looking back on this family adventure, it proved to be instrumental in the future of Longhi's. Our first cook was my daughter Gabrielle, who at age eighteen managed the kitchen for a year. Carol Longhi is currently the chef at Longhi's. She graduated from the Culinary Institute of America in Hyde Park, New York, in 1994. Peter Longhi has worked for the restaurant since he was eighteen, and became the general manager at age twenty. Charlie Longhi's first job, after I asked everybody what they wanted to do, was official food tester. (Charlie was fourteen years old at the time.) Charlie has had several jobs in the restaurant, and is currently a fine musician. Charlie made his musical debut at Longhi's at seventeen and went on to the Berklee School of Music in Boston, where he graduated magna cum laude. The latest addition to the family is my twelve-year-old daughter Genafer, who is the youngest hostess in America.

In 1976 I took fifty people who worked for me on a one-week vacation to Hawaii. My second night in Maui I walked into Captain Jack's Family Restaurant at 888 Front Street in Lahaina. After sitting down to eat I casually asked Captain Jack if he knew of any places for sale. He retorted, "Yes, this building. I've been in Chapter 11 for two years."

As I was a vegetarian at the time, I ordered a Greek salad. When it arrived there was no feta cheese and no Greek olives. I called Jack over and asked, "Where's the feta cheese? Where's the olives?" He said, "Bob, come to my house tomorrow. We'll talk about the building. I've got some imported feta cheese and some kalamata olives, and I'll make you a great Greek salad." I said, "Jack, you know why you're going bankrupt? You keep your feta cheese in the wrong place!" Jack laughed and we made a date for the next day. I decided that night that I wanted to live in Maui and that 888 Front Street would be the perfect place to create my restaurant, Longhi's Cafe. (I later decided to just call it Longhi's.) We met the next day, talked for a few minutes, shook hands, and made a deal. Nine months later Longhi's became a reality.

The Making
of a Restaurant

TWENTY YEARS LATER, Longhi's has become one of the most successful restaurants in the United States. We started with ninety seats, but in 1983 made a major move by expanding to the upstairs and increased our capacity to 250 seats. After being in business for six months we started serving breakfast, and since 1977 we have been serving breakfast, lunch, and dinner seven days a week, almost every day of the year. We have served more than six million people and have grossed more than a hundred million dollars in revenues. For the past ten years we have been one of the two or three top-grossing restaurants in the state of Hawaii.

We've also won numerous awards for our food, service, and wine. Since 1987 we have been the recipient of *Wine Spectator's* yearly Award of Excellence—the only independent restaurant in Hawaii that enjoys this prestigious distinction. We have been the winner of the *Honolulu Advertiser's* Ilima award (which signifies the best restaurant in Maui) three out of nine years; winning in 1996 helped celebrate our twentieth year in business. In 1987 we were one of only 19 restaurants awarded five stars from the *Benenson Guide.* We have had many other accolades bestowed on us over the years, but one that was especially meaningful to me was Cornell University choosing Longhi's to be featured at their hotel school for one week in 1988. Our latest and most prestigious honor was receiving the celebrated Five Star Diamond Award in 1997 from the American Academy of Hospitality Services.

Why have we been so successful? Our number-one goal has always been the welfare of the customer. Longhi's is a place where a customer will have not only a delicious meal and great service—but even more important—a wonderful time. I instill in the minds of the people who work for me that every night is a special event. We want our staff to dress as if they are going to a party, and we want them to treat the customers like they are guests at a fabulous banquet. If a diner walks out of Longhi's saying he had a good meal, we're not satisfied. We want him to feel he had a *great* meal, because if he feels he had a great meal, he is going to come back and he is going to praise us to all the people he meets and knows. When he's on the beaches in Maui, and when he goes back to his hometown, he will expound on what a terrific experience he had at that great restaurant called Longhi's. Because of the wonderful job my staff has done over the years in accomplishing this goal, much of our business at Longhi's comes from people who have been directed here by friends who have had the Longhi's experience.

One of the most unique things about Longhi's is that we have a verbal menu. When people come to eat, the waitperson recites the menu and tells them what we have that day, giving an explanation about all of our food preparations and, oftentimes, even a mini-travelogue. This sometimes takes a little bit longer than in most restaurants, but we have found that people enjoy the experience because it is unique. It also gives them an opportunity to relate to the people who are serving them. Presenting a verbal menu creates an existential mind-set for the server, who has to be totally in the present. My belief is that

a written menu often causes a restaurant's staff to treat their customers in a perfunctory manner. With a verbal menu the staff must be constantly aware of what is happening. If the people who work for you are in the present, it gives them more satisfaction in their jobs and consequently makes them happier. It has rewarded us over the years with a highly intelligent staff, the type of people who *need* to enjoy their work.

We have very few rules at Longhi's. I go to many restaurants where they have these little rules: you can't sit here, you can't sit there, you can't do this or that. At Longhi's, customers can do anything they want. Our main rule is the golden rule: take care of the other person, and treat the other person the way you want to be treated. The only other rules are to make sure you smile, and to keep everybody happy. As for uniforms, I don't believe in them—that's not the way I want to lead my life, and that's not the way I want to run my restaurant.

There are three major things people talk about in restaurants. One is the quality of the food, another is the attentiveness of the service, and the third is atmosphere. My firm belief, obviously, is that you have to have all these, but my major emphasis has always been that food is number one. If you have great food but mediocre service, you're going to be a lot better off than you would be with mediocre food and great service. At Longhi's we have great food, great service, and great atmosphere.

We go all over the world to get our products. Over the years many people have asked me how I can have a great restaurant in the middle of *nowhere*. But they are completely mistaken because we are in the center of *everywhere*. We can go to South America, we can go to Australia, we can go to the mainland, we can go to New Zealand. At any given time around the world, there's summer or there's spring or there's fall.

For example, we have beautiful spring peas continually on our menu, because there's springtime in Chile, New Zealand, and on the U.S. mainland all at different times, so we can always purchase spring peas. We also always have fresh raspberries, blueberries, or blackberries. We had a party in the middle of the winter and we had fresh cherries. I said to the people who were having dinner, "Do you think you can get these fresh cherries on the mainland?" They said, "Are you kidding? No way!" There are not too many restaurants in the world that are willing to do that. We have fresh products at all times. We have fresh basil that we grow locally twelve months a  year. I remember I used to go to great restaurants in New York City that only had fresh basil during the summer because they grew it in their private garden on Long Island. Maui is a place where you can grow anything you want, just about year-round. Many of the ingredients we use in the restaurant are locally grown. If we feel that the locally grown products aren't up to our standards, we then go offshore to get what we need.

At Longhi's we feel that the best steaks come from the Midwest, so instead of using local beef we have our corn-fed beef specially bred for us in Iowa. Consequently, one of the local sayings is, "The best-kept secret in Maui is that Longhi's has the finest and biggest steaks in Hawaii." We not only have great steaks, but we know what to do with them—you'll find several of our many delicious steak recipes in this book.

There is no better fish than Hawaiian fish, and we use primarily local fish caught the same day and served immediately. We buy only enough seafood for each day. Once in a while we will go away from Maui to get special fish, such as salmon flown in from the Pacific Northwest or as far away as Norway.

One of our specialties at Longhi's is lobster. I happen to think that North Atlantic lobsters are the best in the world. Every week we have two hundred to four hundred pounds of lobster flown in by United Airlines. We keep them alive in our tank so we always have fresh lobsters. Very often when we fly in the lobsters, we will also include specialty items from the East Coast, such as soft-shell crabs, littleneck clams, mussels, Block Island sword-fish, and Nantucket scallops. We will go to whatever extremes it takes in order to get the products we want. We serve approximately a thousand meals a day, and when I ask a customer, "How big do you think my freezer is?" the standard answer is, "It must be gigan-

tic." But actually our freezer is extremely small, as we use it for only a few items. Our pastry chef, Randy Ortega, uses the freezer primarily for the fabulous ice creams and sorbets he makes on a daily basis.

At Longhi's we believe food should be served in its freshest state. We don't use pre-cooked brown sauces; almost all the sauces we serve are made to order, which takes two to three minutes. In this way everything a customer orders is made quickly and cooked to perfection without masking it with numerous fancy, heavy sauces. We buy the finest ingredients and try to bring out the best in them without gilding the lily.

The second thing you need in a fine restaurant is terrific service. We feel that the people who work at Longhi's provide excellent service because their attitude is that they are there to please you. We will do anything we can do as long as it's within our abilities.

A top-level restaurant must also have a wonderful atmosphere. One of the reasons people have such a good time at Longhi's is we have duplicated a negative-ion generator. This creates an atmosphere that causes people to feel energetic, happy, and vivacious. Longhi's has an energizing effect. This is achieved by the high ceilings, round corners, and curved archways. All the angles are curved, which enables the air to move freely and not be stagnant. Longhi's is a beautiful restaurant. Our tables are round, we have fresh flowers, and we are close to the Pacific Ocean. These elements all create negative ions. It has been proven that negative ions create a vivifying atmosphere that elevates one's state of mind to a more euphoric level. When you come to Longhi's to dine you are in a restaurant that is on one of the most beautiful islands on the planet. (*Condé Nast Traveler* has picked Maui as the number-one island destination in the world for the past two years.) You walk into a restaurant that is extremely beautiful, one that has a feeling about it that is exciting and fun. You have people who come to wait on you who are vivacious and want to make your experience the best they possibly can. Then you finally end up with fantastic food that's been prepared by people who are into making you a great meal using the best possible ingredients. How can you beat that? Now that's the total experience at Longhi's. In this cookbook, we are going to show you how to achieve these same results at home by using recipes that have proven to be popular for twenty years.

A new rage among restauranteurs is to create a new menu every day. Though that sounds exciting, you can walk in one day and have a wonderful meal, then go back a week later and they no longer have that dish. I believe that when people eat a wonderful dish, they want to have it again. There is a reason things are done classically: *because they work!* So if you come to Longhi's twenty years from now and you order Ahi Torino, you are going to get the same dish you ate twenty years ago. We are one of the few restaurants where you can get the same thing you ordered several years ago and have it prepared at least as well if not better. Over the years we have added many things to our menu and taken off some things, but if you come to Longhi's and you want something you enjoyed in the past but don't hear it on the menu, chances are we can make it for you, because we can make anything. We have excellent cooks, a wonderful kitchen manager, and a fabulous chef, so we can do anything you want as long as we have the ingredients.

Longhi's
Classic Recipes

Pasta

IN MY OPINION the most important food in the world is pasta. Some say the Chinese invented it, some say the Italians—it hardly matters as it is the basic food in many cultures. When people think of China they think of rice, but when one becomes knowledgeable about the many types of Chinese cuisine, ranging from Mandarin to Szechuan to Cantonese, they will discover that in all of these cuisines the Chinese utilize noodles in many of their dishes. Many other Asian and European cultures use noodles of different types. The champion, however, and the world leader in pasta, is Italy. We at Longhi's believe that our pasta dishes are as good as any restaurant's in the world. The reason for this is that we use the best ingredients. We cook everything to order. All of our sauces are fresh, and we serve our pasta perfectly cooked.

About fifteen years ago in California, it became very popular to serve only freshly made pasta. California is a leader in new fads and food inventions. They used freshly made pasta for spaghetti, linguine, ravioli, rigatoni, capellini, and all the different types of noodles. My strong opinion is that homemade pasta is wonderful if you use it for the right thing— stuffed pasta, such as cannelloni, ravioli, or manicotti. It is also excellent for Fettuccine Alfredo. In most other instances I am a one hundred percent believer in using dried pasta imported from Italy. Why? Because in order to enjoy pasta properly, it must be cooked al dente, which means firm to the bite. If you look at most boxes of dried pasta, they will tell you to cook it for 8, 10, or 12 minutes. My experience has been that you are better off cooking it a couple of minutes less; that way the pasta stays firm. When you bite it you can feel the inside core. That inside core is wonderful because great pasta is made with hard durum semolina wheat, and that gives it a whole different character from all other noodles. I've discovered that most Americans cook pasta too long, which tends to make it mushy. The problem with homemade pasta when it is used for spaghetti, linguine, or angel hair is that it can easily become too soft. It doesn't have that firmness. At Longhi's we have one full-time pasta maker, Guy Corti, who has been with us for twenty years. Guy specializes in making all of our stuffed pastas. He uses homemade pasta that he makes on a very small hand-cranked pasta machine. Every day he makes manicotti, several types of cannelloni and ravioli, and other stuffed pasta specialties.

There are three things needed to manufacture great pasta. First, you must have pure water. In Italy there is a province called Abruzzi. This is an area northeast of Rome bordered by the Adriatic. In this province there is a little town called Faro San Martino. Though this town has fewer than 1,500 inhabitants, there are two large, world-famous pasta factories there. Last summer I went to Italy to investigate the Del Verde pasta company because I had heard such good reports about it. While I was having lunch, the president of the company went to the mountain stream and gathered a pitcher of water. When I drank the water I was amazed: it was the greatest water I had ever tasted. It was sweet, tasty, and clear, just fantastic. This is the water they use to make Del Verde pasta.

I have a friend who is a manufacturer of sunglasses. He told me last year he was traveling to the coastal town of Pescara in Abruzzi on the Adriatic Sea. I asked him why he was going there, not many people go to Pescara. He told me that it's one of the only two places in the world, the other being in Japan, that has water that's clear enough and clean enough to properly manufacture their sunglasses.

Next, you have to use hard durum wheat. Abruzzi has the best wheat in the world for making pasta. Del Verde gets all their wheat within 150 miles of where they manufacture their pasta. Finally, the third thing you need is expertise. Del Verde has been in business for thirty years. They have a fantastic plant with modern equipment, but they still use many of the old methods, and they put their heart into it and come up with terrific pasta. In 1993, Food and Wine magazine, in an independent test conducted by ten of the best restauranteurs in New York City, picked Del Verde as their favorite pasta in the world.

When you cook pasta, use a large pot and bring the water to a boil. Then add two tablespoons of olive oil and one teaspoon of salt. Add the pasta to the boiling water, being careful not to break it. The olive oil and salt add taste and prevent the pieces of pasta from sticking together. Use a pasta fork and stir the pasta often so it doesn't stick. Once the pasta is done (and this is determined by tasting it—do not throw it against the wall!), remove the pasta from the boiling water and immediately add it to the sauce. Do not rinse it in water! My mother, who was not a great cook, although she did make fantastic devil's food cakes, always rinsed the pasta with cold water. She told me she did that because she wanted to get rid of the starch. That's the worst thing you can do, because when the starch is still on the pasta it acts as a magnet for the sauce, which adheres to the pasta in a synergistic way. When I hear people say you should get rid of the starch, it doesn't make much sense, because pasta *is* a starch. The best way to handle the pasta once it's cooked is to put it directly into your sauce. Don't be afraid of getting some of the water that the pasta cooked in into the sauce because that water is excellent. What it does is bind and thicken the sauce, in addition to enhancing its taste.

THE MOST BASIC SAUCE in Italian cuisine is a red tomato sauce, called Pomodoro Sauce. There are many ways to make it; some have meat, some do not. This version has no meat. This very simple sauce takes only a few minutes to make but it is wonderful. It can be served on any kind of pasta, from angel hair to rigatoni, and on stuffed pastas such as cannelloni or manicotti

It's also wonderful with chicken or veal Parmesan. You'll find it used in numerous ways in other recipes throughout this book. It's a basic red sauce that should be mastered by anyone who wants to cook Italian-style. You will get terrific satisfaction from making this sauce and serving it to your friends. There is nothing better than a simple bowl of capellini with Pomodoro Sauce and Parmesan cheese.

This sauce is composed of seven ingredients: garlic, olive oil, onions, tomatoes, basil, salt, and pepper. The important thing about this dish is the way you use the garlic. Garlic is so versatile that you will get a different result each time you use it, depending on how it is handled. For this dish we use a garlic press. If you are able to get beautiful, fresh, ripe tomatoes, they are the best. If you can't, my recommendation is to use whole Hunt tomatoes in their juice. We have tested all kinds of tomatoes in our kitchen, including the imported Italian ones, and we have found that Hunts give us the best result. They are extremely consistent, taste wonderful, and will produce a great sauce for you.

After the sauce has been finished and added to the pasta, one of the great ways of enhancing it is to add freshly grated Parmigiano-Reggiano Parmesan cheese. Each year at Longhi's we use $200,000-worth of this great cheese—probably more than any restaurant in the world. One of the reasons we have such great results is that we always use the best ingredients. If you can't get Parmigiano-Reggiano, try to get a Parmesan cheese that you grate yourself or that the grocer will grate for you. Avoid buying prepacked Parmesan cheese.

Pomodoro Sauce

2 (28-ounce) cans whole tomatoes

1 medium onion, cut into $^1/_4$-inch dice

$^1/_2$ cup extra virgin olive oil

4 garlic cloves, pressed through a garlic press

$^1/_4$ cup (about 10 sprigs) fresh basil leaves, chopped

Salt and pepper to taste

■ Drain tomatoes, reserving the juice. Pour tomatoes into a glass bowl and break them up into small pieces. In a saucepan over medium heat, sauté the chopped onion in the olive oil until translucent, about 4 minutes. Add the pressed garlic and sauté 2 minutes. Add the tomatoes and cook for 3 minutes, then stir the reserved tomato juice into the pan. Let simmer for 10 to 20 minutes until saucy. Add basil and season the sauce with salt and pepper to taste. Mix well.

Yields 4 cups

ABOUT PENNE ARRABIATA

FOR THE PAST FIFTEEN YEARS Penne Arrabiata has become one of the world's most popular dishes. Before that, if you went into an Italian restaurant and asked for Arrabiata, most would not have known what you were talking about, and they certainly didn't know how to make it. Now, however, you can walk into almost any Italian restaurant in America—and almost everywhere in Italy—and they will have Penne Arrabiata. The problem is that every place you go you get a different version.

I was first introduced to this dish fifteen years ago by Mama Resta. She was a terrific cook who had a restaurant in Makawao, which is a small cowboy town located on Maui's Haleakala hillside. I loved this dish, one of the tastiest pastas I ever had. For one full year I tried to recreate it, without success. It seems very simple, with only eight ingredients: tomatoes, garlic, hot pepper, olive oil, penne, a little parsley, and some salt and pepper. How can a dish with only these few ingredients vary so much in taste? Finally Mama's son, Piero Resta, a well-known artist who resides on Maui, showed me the secret of this dish, which has to do with the way you cut the garlic and how long you cook it. Garlic gives you a different result depending on how you use it. If you mince it, you get one result; if

you put it in a garlic press, you get another result; and if you slice it, still another. Cooking it for a short time as opposed to a long time again yields a dramatic difference. When you prepare the garlic for Penne Arrabiata, chop it into small pebbles and cook until it is almost burnt! And I literally mean almost burnt! There is a period of about ten seconds—I call it the window of decision—during which you must arrest the cooking just before the garlic burns by adding fresh hot peppers to the pan. When you do this, you will get a smell that is unbelievable. It may take you awhile, but once you recognize this smell and know that you have cooked the garlic perfectly, you will have created a dish fit for anyone's palate, be they a king or a beggar. That is the secret of this dish.

When I was in Italy twelve years ago, traveling with my wife Gail, I asked for Penne Arrabiata in every restaurant we went to. No one made it the way I liked it. We finally arrived in Rome after traveling through Italy for three months. It was our last day and I went to a very famous restaurant called El Pasetto. The owner happened to be there and I said, "You know, I've been looking all over Italy for Penne Arrabiata the way I know it should be cooked." He said, "I can make it for you, I guarantee it." Ten minutes later a wonderful dish arrived with a sauce that was perfect. It was the first time that I had Penne Arrabiata the way I liked it since I left America. That day I had the largest meal of my life. I ate for three hours, while the owner, the manager, and the waiters stood around watching me eat, marveling at my capacity.

This is the perfect dish to help you practice what I call "cooking meditation." Everybody talks about meditating; they go to India, they go to gurus, read books, buy tapes, learn a mantra, do everything they possibly can so they can meditate. In my opinion true meditation is being completely in the present, and when you make this dish you *must* be in the present. Your mind cannot wander—you cannot be watching television or talking with your friends. You must watch the garlic so it doesn't burn, although if you don't cook it enough, you won't get the right flavor. Another thing to remember with this dish is to always keep the heat high. Arrabiata means "agitated," so use high heat throughout the cooking. Put all your attention into the dish, and when you are finished and have done it properly, you will have one of the great dishes of all time. People will call you a great cook just based on this one dish. Good luck.

Penne Arrabiata

1 teaspoon salt

Dash of olive oil

1 pound penne pasta

1 (28-ounce) can whole tomatoes

18 cloves garlic, chopped

$^1/_2$ cup extra virgin olive oil

1 to 2 hot chile peppers (red, green, or yellow), chopped

$^1/_2$ cup chopped parsley (optional)

Salt and freshly ground pepper

▓ Boil water in a large stainless steel pot. Add 1 teaspoon salt and a dash of olive oil to the water, then add the penne. Drain the canned tomatoes, reserving the juice.

▓ In a saucepan over high heat, sauté the chopped garlic in the extra virgin olive oil. (Make sure the oil is hot before adding the garlic, which should sizzle when it hits the pan.) Sauté the garlic until it is very brown but not burned. At this point, just before the garlic is ready to burn, add the chopped hot peppers, wait 10 to 20 seconds, then stir in the tomatoes, keeping the heat high. Cut the tomatoes into quarters to release the juices. Simmer for a few minutes, stirring often. Add reserved tomato juice and cook a few minutes longer.

▓ When the penne are cooked al dente, scoop them from the water directly into the sauce. Add the chopped parsley and mix well. Turn off the heat and add salt and pepper to taste.

Serves 4

ABOUT SPAGHETTI PUTANA

PASTA PUTANA, a dish I created for my cooking show, has become a very popular item at Longhi's. It's a wonderful dish for you to make for your family and friends, and is especially fun if you are having a small dinner party. The inspiration for this recipe comes from the classic dish Puttanesca, which loosely translates to "hooker's pasta," and was created in Italy by the women of the night in a section of Rome called Trastevere. They had to have a sauce that could be made quickly, because at any given moment they might have some business. The dish also had to be spicy and energizing—they didn't want a dish that would put them to sleep or have a soporific effect. This dish had to be exciting and it had to be titillating. Puttanesca has become popular throughout the world. You can go to any Italian restaurant and you will find Puttanesca.

I decided to create a dish like Puttanesca but with some variations. In the classic rendition Romano cheese is used to flavor the dish. (Romano, as the name might suggest, is very popular in Rome.) I decided to use feta cheese instead, having discovered that feta works extremely well with pasta. It melts well and its flavor enhances the taste.

Another change I made to this dish was the use of the garlic. A classic Puttanesca includes two or three chopped cloves of garlic. In my version, I sauté 20 to 25 whole cloves of garlic for

about 6 minutes or until they are soft and golden. The first time I tried this dish I was amazed: the result was terrific! A dish was created that has become very popular in my restaurant. I did some research to find out what the name for Puttanesca was in Greek. I discovered that this word is Putana, so we call this dish Putana—dedicated to the women of the night in Athens.

When you read this recipe and you see that it calls for 25 cloves of garlic, I am sure your first reaction will be, "How can anybody use that much garlic? It will overwhelm you!" Believe me, it doesn't. The garlic takes on a nutty, mellow flavor. It's wonderful. Try it. I'm sure you will be very happy with this dish.

Spaghetti Putana

12 oil-packed anchovies

1/2 cup milk

1 teaspoon salt

Dash of olive oil

1 pound spaghetti

1 (28-ounce) can whole tomatoes

25 whole garlic cloves, peeled

1/2 cup extra virgin olive oil

1 or 2 hot green or red chile peppers, chopped

18 Siciliano olives

18 black Greek olives

1/2 cup coarsely chopped parsley

1/2 cup feta cheese, crumbled

Salt and freshly ground black pepper

≈

■ Fill a large stainless steel pot with water and bring to a boil. Place the anchovies in a bowl and cover with milk to soak. When the water boils, add 1 teaspoon salt and a dash of olive oil, then drop in the spaghetti. Drain the canned tomatoes, reserving the juice. Drain the anchovies, rinse in cool water, and chop.

■ In a saucepan over medium heat, sauté the 25 whole garlic cloves in the olive oil for about 5 minutes. Add the chopped anchovies and cook 1 minute. Mix in the chopped hot peppers, cook 1 minute, and add the olives. Then add the tomatoes, cutting each one in quarters to release the juices. Sauté 5 minutes. Add the reserved tomato juice and simmer a few minutes longer.

■ When the pasta is cooked al dente, scoop it directly from the water into the sauce. Add the chopped parsley and crumbled feta cheese and mix well. Remove from heat and add salt and pepper to taste.

Serves 4

LAST YEAR I WAS PLANNING a Valentine's Day benefit for the Kapalua Art School. I was looking for a new pasta creation that would set the theme for the party. My girlfriend DeBorah suggested a recipe that I make with garlic, olive oil, and anchovies that is a classic dish in Italy. I wanted to make something different, something that had a terrific amount of excitement to it. I also wanted a dish that would be very hot and energize the eater. So I combined four basic ingredients that one would not think could work well together, but the result was terrific. These four are garlic, anchovies, hot pepper, and feta cheese. Each of these ingredients is very pungent, strong, and distinctive in its own right. But when cooked together in hot olive oil, a miracle happened; the four neutralized each other and created a flavor that is unique and extremely tasty. The dish also had a certain hotness to it that got people excited. After I finished cooking it, DeBorah said, "You know, Bob, we should call this dish Pasta Amore," which means pasta for lovers. And indeed, my advice to you, gentlemen, is that if you want to cook for a woman, invite her to your place and make Pasta Amore (it takes less than ten minutes). I guarantee you will have a wonderful night!

Pasta Amore

15 oil-packed anchovies

¹/₂ cup milk

1 teaspoon salt

Dash of olive oil

1 pound spaghetti

Juice from 1 (28-ounce) can whole tomatoes

15 cloves garlic, chopped

¹/₂ cup extra virgin olive oil

3 hot chile peppers, diced

¹/₂ cup feta cheese

Parsley, chopped

Salt and pepper

■ Soak the anchovies in the milk for at least 10 minutes, then set aside.

■ Fill a large stainless steel pot with water and bring to a boil. Add 1 teaspoon salt and a dash of olive oil, then drop the spaghetti into the boiling water.

■ Drain the canned tomatoes, reserving the juice. (Save tomatoes for another use.) Drain the anchovies, rinse in cool water, and chop.

■ In a pan over medium heat, sauté the garlic in the extra virgin olive oil until golden brown. Add anchovies and sauté for 30 seconds, then add the diced hot peppers and sauté for 2 to 3 minutes. Add the tomato juice and cook the sauce a few minutes. When the spaghetti is cooked al dente, add it to the sauce in the pan and stir in the feta cheese, tossing the mixture well. Mix in the parsley and add salt and pepper to taste.

Serves 4

I LOVE THIS SAUCE for its simple and savory flavor. It is quick to make, and so satisfying and versatile that it can be served with any kind of pasta.

Capellini with Tomato and Basil

1 (28-ounce) can whole canned tomatoes

6 garlic cloves, peeled and pressed

$1/2$ cup extra virgin olive oil

1 teaspoon salt

1 tablespoon olive oil

1 pound capellini

10 sprigs fresh basil

$1/2$ cup Parmigiano-Reggiano or other Parmesan cheese

Salt and freshly ground black pepper

▪ Fill a large stainless steel pot with water and bring to a boil. Drain the tomatoes, reserving the juice in a bowl. In a saucepan over medium heat, sauté 3 cloves of the pressed garlic in the olive oil. Quarter the tomatoes, and add to the pan. Cook for 5 minutes, then add reserved tomato juice and continue to cook over medium heat for 3 to 5 minutes, or until thick and bubbling.

▪ Add salt and 1 tablespoon olive oil to the boiling water, then drop in the capellini. Cook 2 minutes until al dente. Scoop capellini directly from the water into the pan with the tomato sauce. Add fresh basil and mix well. Press the remaining 3 garlic cloves into the pasta. Add the Parmigiano cheese and mix over low heat for 1 minute. Add salt and pepper to taste.

Serves 4

ABOUT MACARONI AND CHEESE

WHAT DISH IS COOKED most often at home by American mothers and fathers? I think the answer has to be macaroni and cheese. It's usually made with American cheese and elbow macaroni, and most often is baked in the oven. It's a wonderful dish, it has fed many people, and many Americans have been brought up on it. This recipe, however, is a brand-new version of macaroni and cheese. I was thinking about macaroni and cheese one day and I thought, well, it's a wonderful dish, but it could use a little more excitement. So I sat down and created what I call Longhi's Quintessential Macaroni and Cheese.

I've featured this dish in my television show and gotten tremendous feedback from people who have tried it and loved it. This dish is exciting, but it's also a meal you can give to your family and your children. Even little kids seem to love it. We use the basic ingredients for macaroni and cheese but then vary it a little by using olive oil, garlic, anchovies, and tomatoes. When you make the classic macaroni and cheese, by the time you get it out of the oven you may have been cooking it for up to an hour. You can prepare this version in less than half an hour and have something with a new twist to it that your family will like.

The first secret is to cut the garlic in paper-thin slivers, which is called amandine-style. I like to use two types of cheese in this recipe: mild cheddar and Monterey jack. For my macaroni I prefer long ziti. This pasta is difficult to

find, very few manufacturers still make long ziti, but Del Verde is one of the pasta companies that does. It comes in a beautiful box and it's very unusual. I find that kids like it a lot because they can suck it up and have fun with it while they are eating. You also can use other pasta like perciatelli, penne, shells, or even rigatoni. Try to get a pasta with some weight and body to it. Don't use capellini or spaghettini or any kind of thin delicate pasta.

This is an example of a dish where you can use your imagination. You may not like to use cheddar or Monterey jack; you may have some other cheese you prefer. You can use any type of cheese with this, just make sure you use a cheese that melts well (most cheeses do). The last thing you will do is to add a little bit of ground cayenne pepper. Cayenne can be very hot, so you must be judicious with it, depending on what your family likes. My daughter Genafer doesn't like hot things, so I never use cayenne pepper when I make this dish for her. Use your imagination and make small changes if you want. My advice to you is to try this recipe once as written, see how you like it, and go from there. I hope you enjoy it. I certainly do.

Longhi's Quintessential Macaroni and Cheese

12 oil-packed anchovies

1/2 cup milk

1 teaspoon salt

Dash of olive oil

1 pound ziti pasta

1 (28-ounce) can whole tomatoes

15 cloves garlic, slivered

1/2 cup extra virgin olive oil

1/2 pound Monterey jack cheese, shredded

1/2 pound mild cheddar cheese, shredded

1 teaspoon ground cayenne pepper to taste

Salt and freshly ground black pepper to taste

■ Soak the anchovies in milk for at least 15 minutes. Fill a large stainless steel pot with water and bring to a boil. Add salt and a dash of olive oil, and immediately drop in the ziti. Drain the tomatoes, reserving the juice. Drain the anchovies, rinse them in cool water, and chop.

■ In a saucepan over medium heat, sauté the garlic in the extra virgin olive oil for 1 to 2 minutes. Add the anchovies and sauté 1 minute. Quarter the tomatoes and add to the pan. Add the reserved tomato juice and simmer the sauce for 5 minutes. Mix in shredded cheeses. Add the cayenne pepper. When the pasta is cooked al dente, scoop it into the sauce and mix well. Finish with salt and pepper.

Serves 4

ABOUT FETTUCCINE ALFREDO

IN THE 1930s Mary Pickford and Douglas Fairbanks were visiting Rome and stopped to have dinner at Alfredo Restaurant. Alfredo at that time was certainly not world famous, but he was well known in Rome for his creative fettuccine preparation. The unique part about the dish was that he used golden spoons to toss the pasta in front of the customer. Mary and Douglas loved it so much they started raving about it, and after Alfredo served his dish at the 1939 World's Fair in New York, fettuccine Alfredo became world famous. This is a dish that anybody can make. It only has a few ingredients—but it has a big *If*. And that *If* is, *If* you use the best ingredients, you will get a terrific fettuccine Alfredo. Many restaurants in America and all over the world have fettuccine Alfredo on their menu. Unfortunately most of the fettuccine Alfredo that you will eat is not made the way it was by Signor Alfredo for Mary Pickford and Douglas Fairbanks back in the 1930s.

We believe that Longhi's fettuccine Alfredo is superlative, the equal of any rendition one can find in Italy, including Alfredo in Rome. The reason is that we use only the best ingredients. Four things are needed to make fettuccine Alfredo. One, you must have excellent butter. Two, you must have high-grade fresh heavy cream. Third and most important, you must use Parmigiano-Reggiano cheese—not Romano, and not the canned grated cheese you find in the supermarket. Obviously, in order to make the dish properly you must also have excellent noodles. You can use homemade noodles, which are delicious when they are made right. You can also buy dried fettuccine noodles from an Italian manufacturer and get wonderful results. This is a dish that I do not recommend cooking al dente. I believe that fettuccine noodles should be softer than other pastas.

Once you have mastered the sauce for fettuccine Alfredo, you can create some wonderful variations. We have a dish at Longhi's called fettuccine Lombardi. This is fettuccine Alfredo with fresh spring peas and thinly sliced prosciutto added. (I personally like it without the prosciutto, with just the fresh spring peas.) Another variation is to add shrimp. You can see that you can do many different things with it. It is an exciting sauce, although it is highly caloric, so I recommend that you don't eat it every night, but save it for a special occasion. Nothing can beat fettuccine Alfredo or especially fettuccine Alfredo with fresh peas.

Fettuccine Alfredo

1 teaspoon salt

Dash of olive oil

1 pound fettuccine (fresh or dried)

$^1/_2$ stick ($^1/_4$ cup) sweet butter

3 cups fresh heavy cream

1 cup Parmigiano-Reggiano cheese,
   grated

Black pepper

Nutmeg

■ Fill a large stainless steel pot with water and bring to a boil. Add salt and a dash of olive oil, then drop the fettuccine into the boiling water. Cook until done, and drain.

■ In a wide, flat pan over medium heat, add butter and $2^1/_2$ cups of the cream. When the butter has melted and the liquid starts to make small bubbles, simmer for 1 more minute. Add fettuccine to the pan and toss over low heat; simmer 2 minutes. Add the cheese, the remaining $^1/_2$ cup of cream, 4 to 6 twists of freshly milled pepper, and a quick grating of nutmeg. Toss the mixture well, making sure each strand of pasta is coated. Serve immediately.

Serves 4

Variation:

Fettuccine Lombardi

$^1/_2$ cup fresh peas, shelled

$^1/_3$ cup thinly sliced prosciutto, cut
   into $^1/_4$-inch-wide, 1-inch-long strips

■ Steam, blanch, or sauté the peas. When the sauce is ready, just before you add the fettuccine, add the peas and prosciutto. Cook 30 seconds, then add the pasta, mix well, and serve.

THIS PASTA IS VERY REFRESHING. The creamy smoothness is offset by the tangy zest of the lemon. It is especially satisfying at lunch or for a light dinner.

Zucchini-Lemon Pasta

1 tablespoon salt

1 pound linguine

1 teaspoon chopped garlic

$1/2$ cup dry white wine

$1/4$ cup fresh lemon juice

Zest of 1 lemon

1 cup heavy cream

2 tablespoons salted butter

2 small zucchini, julienned

Salt

Freshly ground black pepper

■ Fill a large stockpot with water and bring to a boil. Add salt, then drop the linguine into the boiling water. Cook until al dente, and drain.

■ While pasta is cooking, combine garlic, wine, and lemon juice and zest in a large sauté pan with high sides and reduce until 2 tablespoons remain, about 5 minutes. Add the cream and simmer for 1 minute.

■ In a saucepan, melt the butter over medium-low heat. Add the zucchini and sweat for 1 minute.

■ Add the cooked pasta to the cream mixture. Add the zucchini and toss. Season generously with salt and pepper.

Serves 4

HOMEMADE PASTA is perfect for this dish, though you can use the Italian dry pasta sheets made by Delverde if you don't have the time to make your own. Just cook them as directed on the package.

Manicotti

1 cup shredded mozzarella

1 cup shredded provolone

2 cups ricotta

$^1/_2$ cup grated Parmesan cheese

$^1/_4$ teaspoon ground white pepper

Pinch ground black pepper

8 homemade or dried imported Italian cannelloni pasta squares, cooked al dente (page 47)

2 cups warm Besciamella Sauce (page 47)

1 cup warm Pomodoro Sauce (page 23)

■ Mix cheeses and white and black pepper in a bowl until blended. Divide the mixture into 8 portions. Spoon the filling in a line down the middle of each pasta square. Wrap the pasta around the filling and slightly flatten the rolls. Steam the manicotti for 5 minutes, or until hot. Put 2 manicotti on each plate and top with Besciamella Sauce. Add a stripe of Pomodoro Sauce down the center of each plate.

Serves 4

Opposite page: Manicotti

YOU CAN USE EITHER LOBSTER or crabmeat in this recipe with equally excellent results. We originally made these crustacean cannelloni with only crabmeat. After we started bringing lobsters in from Boston, many of our customers and employees felt that lobster cannelloni would also be a great menu item. They were right! It's a fabulous dish and a big-time seller.

Lobster Cannelloni

$^1/_2$ cup shredded mozzarella

$^1/_2$ cup shredded provolone

1 cup ricotta

2 tablespoons grated Parmigiano-Reggiano

$1^1/_2$ cups lobster or crabmeat

Black pepper

8 homemade or premade cannelloni pasta squares, cooked al dente (page 47)

2 cups warm Besciamella Sauce (page 47)

2 tablespoons chopped flat-leaf parsley

■ Mix cheeses together in a bowl, then add the lobster or crabmeat. Mix lightly and add 8 twists of freshly milled pepper. Divide the filling into eight portions. Spoon the filling in a line down the middle of each pasta square. Wrap the pasta around the filling and slightly flatten the rolls. Steam the cannelloni for about 5 minutes, or until hot. Top with Besciamella Sauce and sprinkle with chopped parsley.

Serves 4

ABOUT SPAGHETTI WITH PORCINI MUSHROOMS

THROUGHOUT TUSCANY, Piedmont, Lombardy, and all of northern Italy, porcini mushrooms are at their peak in September, October, and November. You can do many things with porcini—grill them, sauté them, or add them to risotto. One of the best uses of these mushrooms is to make a sauce and serve it with pasta. At Longhi's we always have dried imported porcini from Italy on hand. This sauce is best with fresh porcini, if you can purchase them, but I feel that the dried mushrooms are almost as good as the fresh ones. They reconstitute extremely well and give you a result very close to the fresh. It's one of my favorite dishes.

To accompany this dish, we prefer to use a fruitier wine such as white Zinfandel. But use your imagination and experiment with wines that have different degrees of dryness. Also, porcini have a distinctive flavor, therefore you may want to use more or less of these fungi depending on your taste.

Spaghetti with Porcini Mushrooms

4 ounces dried porcini, rehydrated in wine, or $1/2$ pound fresh porcini, sliced
$1/2$ cup white wine (for soaking porcini), plus $3/4$ cup
1 teaspoon salt
Dash of olive oil
1 pound spaghetti
1 stick ($1/2$ cup) salted butter
$1/4$ cup heavy cream
$1/4$ cup chopped flat-leaf parsley
Salt and freshly ground black pepper

■ Soak the porcini in $1/2$ cup white wine for 30 minutes or until they have absorbed most of the wine.

■ Fill a large stainless steel pot with water and bring to a boil. Add 1 teaspoon salt and a dash of olive oil, then drop the spaghetti into the boiling water and cook until barely al dente, about 5 or 6 minutes.

■ Sauté the porcini in butter for 3 minutes. Add $3/4$ cup dry white wine, cook off the alcohol, then add the heavy cream. Add the cooked pasta to sauce and toss well, then mix in the parsley, salt, and pepper.

Serves 4

AFTER WE HAD INTRODUCED Frutti di Mare (see page 50), many customers asked if we could combine it with pasta. We did some research and decided to create a new dish called Siciliano. When I was in Sicily in 1984, in the beautiful and elegant town of Taormina overlooking the Ionian Sea, I noted that the Sicilians, who use squid in many of their dishes, especially liked serving it with pasta. We took the basic recipe for Frutti di Mare and decided to limit it to squid. We also added hot red peppers, as we discovered that people who enjoy squid like it spicy. This addition has been extremely popular, and is a favorite with our Japanese clientele.

Pasta Siciliano

BOUILLON

1 bay leaf

1 celery stalk, chopped

1 onion, chopped

Juice of 1 lemon

1 teaspoon salt

5 peppercorns

2 to 3 sprigs flat-leaf parsley

SQUID MIXTURE

2 pounds squid, cleaned (see box, opposite page)

$1/4$ cup dry Marsala

$1/4$ cup sweet Marsala

$1/2$ small onion, diced

1 teaspoon minced garlic

$1/4$ cup extra virgin olive oil

$1/2$ teaspoon dried oregano or 1 teaspoon fresh oregano

2 teaspoons salt

1 teaspoon black pepper

1 cup spicy Sicilian whole olives

$3/4$ cup roasted red mancini peppers, julienned

1 tablespoon olive oil

1 pound dried linguine

1 teaspoon crushed red pepper flakes

3 cups warm Pomodoro Sauce (page 23)

$1/4$ cup chopped basil

■ Fill a stockpot with water. Add the bay leaf, celery, onion, lemon juice, salt, peppercorns, and parsley. Cook over medium heat for 20 minutes. Strain and return the liquid to the stovetop, decreasing the heat to low so that the liquid is just barely simmering. Add the cleaned squid and poach for 2 to 3 minutes. While the squid is poaching, prepare an ice bath by filling a large bowl with ice and adding just enough water to cover. Drain squid and shock in the ice bath. Cut squid into $1/4$-inch rings, leaving the tentacles whole.

■ Combine the Marsalas. In a bowl, combine the diced onion, minced garlic, extra virgin olive oil, $1/4$ cup of the combined Marsala, oregano, 1 teaspoon of the salt, and the black pepper. Add the squid, olives, and mancini peppers and toss. This mixture can be used immediately or can hold in the refrigerator for up to 24 hours.

■ Fill a large stainless steel stockpot with water and bring to a boil. Add the remaining 1 teaspoon salt and 1 tablespoon olive oil, then drop in the linguine.

■ In a large sauté pan over medium heat, add $1/2$ cup Marsala and the crushed red pepper flakes. Cook 2 to 3 minutes until reduced by half. Add squid mixture to pan and heat through. Add 3 cups Pomodoro Sauce and mix well for another minute until hot. Mix in chopped basil. When the linguine is cooked al dente, scoop it directly into sauce, toss, and serve.

Serves 4

CLEANING SQUID

If the squid are fresh, put them in cold water to wash them. If they are frozen, defrost them slowly in a bowl in the refrigerator for about 24 hours. When the squid are soft, you can clean them.

Lay the squid on a cutting board, and with a sharp knife cut the tentacles off just below the eyes. The ink sac lies just below the eyes. Discard the eyes and ink sac unless you want to save the ink for other uses. (Some cooks like to use the ink in pasta sauces or risotto. If you are saving the ink, have a small glass ready to collect it by piercing the sac with a needle and gently squeezing the ink into the glass.) Squeeze the top of the tentacles to expel the mouth, a round, hard object that is not good to eat. Discard the mouth and put the tentacles in a bowl of cold water.

Place the remaining sacs on the cutting board. Squeeze the sacs or push down on them with the blunt end of a chef's knife or the palm of your hand to expel the innards and the long cuttlebone. If the cuttlebone does not come out, reach in and pull it out. Now wash the sacs and tentacles in cold water.

YOU CAN USE A VARIETY of mussels in this dish. Make sure the mussels are well scrubbed, and their beards removed, before cooking. We use mussels from primarily three locations: the East Coast, the West Coast, and New Zealand. From the East Coast, we get wild Maine blue mussels, which can be difficult to clean and can vary in size. We also like cultivated farm mussels from Maine, which are more consistent in size but a little smaller, and the rope-cultivated variety from Prince Edward Island. These are the premiere mussels from the East Coast of North America. Even though all three are available year round, they spawn from May to July, and their quality is inferior during these months. The highest quality mussels from the West Coast are found in Washington State. We prefer the Penn Cove variety. These taste best from August to April and are also rope grown. Kamilche mussels from Washington are also excellent. Another mussel worth considering is the Santa Barbara wild variety. New Zealand's seasons are the opposite of ours, so when our mussels are spawning, theirs are in prime condition. We often use New Zealand green lip mussels during the summer months.

Mussels Marinara

3 pounds mussels

Dash of olive oil

$^1/_2$ teaspoon salt

1 pound dried linguine

$^1/_4$ cup sweet Marsala wine

$^1/_4$ cup dry Marsala wine

$^1/_2$ teaspoon crushed hot red pepper flakes

$^1/_4$ cup chopped basil

3 cups warm Pomodoro Sauce (page 23)

■ Pull the beards off the mussels. Rinse the mussels in cool water, soak them for 15 minutes, drain, and rinse again.

■ Fill a large stainless steel stockpot with water and bring to a vigorous boil. Add olive oil and salt. Add the linguine, stirring occasionally to prevent sticking.

■ In a pan over medium heat, add the Marsala, hot pepper flakes, basil, and mussels. Cover the pan and steam mussels until the shells open, about 3 minutes. Remove the mussels from the pan and stir in the heated Pomodoro Sauce; mix well. Let simmer 5 minutes. When linguine is al dente, scoop pasta directly into the sauce and toss. Add the mussels back to the pan, then pour into a large serving dish.

Serves 4

ABOUT LOBSTER LONGHI

IN 1987 MY SON CHARLIE graduated from the famous Berklee School of Music in Boston, Massachusetts. Charlie had been telling me about the great Italian food in North Boston. He especially liked a restaurant called the Daily Catch. He said they had the most fantastic lobster dish that he ever ate. So I said to Charlie, let's go and try it. The dish, called Lobster Fra Diavolo, was prepared in a unique style. I thought it was a wonderful dish and said, after watching how they made it, I'm going back to Maui and hopefully I can make this dish even better. This dish has become very famous at Longhi's, and in fact is one of our top sellers. In my normal egomaniac style, I renamed it Lobster Longhi.

This creation not only has lobster in it, but also mussels, clams, prawns, and squid. You can add scallops or any seafood that you like, although I would recommend that you stay away from fish and use only crustaceans and shellfish. At Longhi's we use two $1\frac{1}{2}$-pound Maine lobsters along with the other seafood.

Lobster Longhi can be eaten by anyone, but if you are squeamish, it may be difficult for you to cook this dish. The secret is to take the fresh lobsters while they are still alive, literally rip them apart, and put the pieces directly into hot olive oil. When I first added this recipe to our menu, one of my cooks absolutely refused to make it!

≈

This dish was originally made with dry white wine. I felt that a wine with a fruitier taste would give the dish a more unique flavor and add to the total excitement, so at Longhi's we use white Zinfandel, which has enough sweetness to cause the dish to really blossom. If you would like to have a meal which will be one of the most memorable you'll ever eat, go to the Daily Catch in Boston and try it. If you are in Maui, come to Longhi's and try our version. I know you will be more than satisfied with either one, and it will be something you will remember for the rest of your life. If you are an adventurous cook, you can make this dish at home. It's not difficult to make—just follow the instructions, and again you will be the hit of the neighborhood.

Lobster Longhi

16 Pacific Manila or 8 littleneck clams

8 mussels

4 whole squid

2 1¹/₂-pound Maine lobsters

11 cloves garlic, chopped

¹/₃ cup extra virgin olive oil

1 to 2 hot red peppers, chopped

4 large shrimp (¹/₃ pound), deveined, shells left on

¹/₂ cup white Zinfandel

¹/₂ cup fish stock (optional)

2 cups warm Pomodoro Sauce (page 23)

1 teaspoon salt

1 tablespoon olive oil

1 pound linguine

- Rinse clams in cool water, soak 15 minutes, drain, and rinse again. Pull the beards off the mussels and rinse in cool water, soak 15 minutes, drain, and rinse again. Clean squid (see instructions, page 41). Save the tentacles for the sauce; cut the body into ¹/₄-inch rings.

- Insert the blade of a chef's knife into each lobster where the tail meets the body; press down and the tail will separate from the body. Hold the body and tear the claws off; with the knife smash each claw where the meat is. Split the tail in half lengthwise.

- In a large sauté pan (14 inches in diameter with 4-inch-high sides), sauté the garlic in the extra virgin olive oil over medium heat; do not let it brown. Add the chopped hot peppers and sauté 30 seconds. Add the lobster pieces to the pan and cook 30 seconds. Add the shrimp, clams, and mussels. Add the white wine and fish stock and cover, shaking the pan occasionally, until the shells open, about 3 minutes. Add the squid and cook 30 seconds. Add the Pomodoro Sauce; mix thoroughly and let simmer 1 minute. Remove seafood from sauce and reserve, while keeping the sauce warm.

- Fill a large stockpot with water and bring to a boil over high heat. Add salt, olive oil, and linguine. Stir well so pasta does not stick.

- Add cooked pasta to the sauce and toss to coat evenly. Transfer the sauced pasta to a large platter and surround with seafood.

Serves 4

THE ITALIANS ARE MASTERS at combining seafood and pasta. A dish you will find throughout Italy, whether you are in Sicily or Venice, is called Vongole Veraci—which, simply translated, means fresh clams in the shell with pasta. In Italy the most popular pasta to use with this dish is linguine.

Throughout Italy you will find this dish made basically the same way, though the clams will vary depending on the location. The clams from the Bari district of the Adriatic are different from those of the Venetian area of the Adriatic, and the clams from the Genoa area of the Mediterranean are different from those of the Naples area. But the dish always has the same basic quality, which is pasta cooked al dente with a sauce made with olive oil, garlic, and clams. (Some versions have red sauce, some do not. When you go into an Italian restaurant you can ask for either *bianco* or *rossa*. I like it either way.) The one thing to be aware of if you eat this dish in Italy is to make sure to taste the dish before you add salt, as the sea salt from the clams is very strong.

Many American restaurants serve what they call pasta with clam sauce. To my taste it is not a great dish because they usually use canned minced clams instead of fresh clams and combine them with some kind of a cream sauce. This dish has merit on its own, but it certainly is not Vongole Veraci, and would not be served in Italy or at Longhi's.

Linguine with Clams (Vongole Veraci)

3 pounds clams

2 tablespoons olive oil

$^1/_2$ teaspoon salt

1 pound dried linguine

$^1/_4$ cup extra virgin olive oil

5 cloves garlic, minced

1 cup white wine

3 tablespoons lemon juice

$^1/_4$ cup chopped flat-leaf parsley

1 cup chopped fresh tomatoes (optional)

4 tablespoons cold butter, cut into
    4 chunks (optional)

■ Clean clams by soaking them in water for 20 minutes to remove sand. Rinse under clear, cool water.

■ Fill a large stockpot with water and bring to a boil. Add olive oil, salt, and linguine. Stir occasionally to prevent sticking. Immediately start clam sauce.

■ Coat a saucepan generously with the olive oil and place over medium-high heat. Sauté the garlic for 1 minute. Add clams, white wine, and lemon juice; cover and steam until clams start to open, about 3 minutes. Add tomatoes, mix into pan, and cover until all the clams are open. Mix in the parsley. Remove the clams from the pan with a slotted spoon. Stir butter chunks into the sauce one at a time until melted. When pasta is al dente, remove from water and add directly to pan. Toss well and pour into serving bowl; top with clams.

Serves 4

Homemade Pasta

¹/₂ cup all-purpose flour

¹/₂ cup bread flour

¹/₂ cup semolina flour

2 eggs

▓ Mix ingredients in a bowl until soft. Roll out dough using a pasta machine set to the widest setting. Keep putting the pasta through the machine, with the die setting getting progressively smaller. Finally, put the pasta dough through the smallest setting. The pasta should be thin. Cut the sheet into two 10 x 14-inch squares.

▓ Fill a large stainless steel pot with water and bring it to a boil. Drop in the pasta sheets and boil for 20 minutes. Remove from the water, drain, and cut each sheet into 4 squares each.

Yields eight 5 x 7-inch squares

Besciamella Sauce

¹/₂ cup butter

¹/₄ onion, sliced

Bay leaf

¹/₄ teaspoon ground white pepper

Black pepper

Nutmeg

¹/₂ teaspoon flour

1 cup heavy cream

1 cup milk

1 tablespoon Parmesan cheese

▓ In a large pot over low to medium heat, melt the butter and sauté the onion until it is translucent; do not let it brown. Add the bay leaf, white pepper and a few twists of freshly milled black pepper, and a scant grating of nutmeg. Add flour and mix well. Whisk in the heavy cream, milk, and Parmesan cheese. Mix until the liquid thickens over medium heat. When the sauce is thick, remove from heat, strain, and return to pan. If the sauce is too thick at this point, add a little milk.

Yields 2 cups

Fish and Seafood

MY NUMBER-ONE FAVORITE exotic seafood is eel from the waters near Venice, Italy. Although they are available year round, Venetian eels are at their peak in September, October, and November. These eels are not from freshwater nor are they from salt water, but live in water that is a mixture of the two. The freshwater comes from the land and the salt water from the ocean. It is only in the area where the two meet that these eels can sustain themselves. From Venice to Bari one can find some of the most thrilling seafood-eating experiences, sampling the larder from the Adriatic Sea. Rimini, Pesaro, Ancona, Pescara, and Bari evoke thoughts of the ubiquitous brodetto, a kind of bouillabaisse that can only be made with the indigenous seafood of the Adriatic.

Another area with great seafood is along the Mediterranean west coast of Italy, including the Ligurian, Tuscan, and Amalfi coasts. The fishermen on the islands of Capri and Ischia do fantastic things with seafood, utilizing all the wonderful frutti di mare found in these magnificent waters. People ask me why I like Italy so much. I tell them that Italy reminds me of a large garden where everything growing is magnificent, and is surrounded by beautiful lakes and ponds stocked with every conceivable delicacy that one can imagine. These treasures range from scaly fish to crustaceans to many other types of creatures that few people have ever seen or heard of—but by some miracle, the people who live in this area know how to make them taste so fantastic that you want to have more and more and more.

Another great area for unsurpassed seafood is the east coast of Spain south of Barcelona. In this area, which borders the western side of the Mediterranean, the Spaniards have a unique way of cooking that is similar to the Italians but has its own distinctiveness. Yet another is Chile, whose cooks take advantage of the Pacific Ocean's wealth of seafood. New Zealand and Australia are also renowned for the terrifically varied seafood available in these areas.

We now come to Hawaii. I believe that the Hawaiian waters, in spite of their paucity of crustaceans, do have the finest ocean fish. The waters in Hawaii are extremely clear. They do not suffer from the pollution that has marred many of the planet's oceans. Even though many people live in Hawaii, and many more people visit us, there is an extremely abundant inventory of different fish. Most of the fish we use at Longhi's is locally caught and served within one day of the time that we buy it. Many of the fish have exotic names, such as ono, onaga, opakapaka, uku, leihi, shutome, ahi, and the ubiquitous mahimahi, and over the years we have served all of them. The recipes on the following pages are the ones we use to cook these various creatures so that their full flavors are enhanced. Follow them and you will be able to get the very best results when cooking these fish.

In addition to local seafood, we serve many different kinds of crustaceans. We fly our lobsters in from Maine. We use Nova Scotia hard shell lobsters, which I feel are the best. We fly our clams and mussels in from various places such as Washington State, Cape Cod, Australia, and New Zealand. We fly in swordfish from Block Island. We fly these various products in only when they are in season and in their peak condition. During the spring we have live softshell crab for a period of about two months. Oftentimes we will procure live Dungeness crab from the coast of California. We use Nantucket scallops or else go to other places around the world where scallops are in season. All of these seafood items can be served broiled, steamed, or sautéed. The Italians are masters of marrying seafood with pasta, so at Longhi's we have myriad pasta dishes featuring different types of seafood. We have Vongole Veraci, which is linguine with fresh clams, one of the greatest dishes you will ever taste. We have pasta with mussels, pasta with lobster, pasta with squid. One of our most famous dishes, Lobster Longhi, incorporates every one of the crustaceans.

At Longhi's we serve seafood in a traditional manner, such as grilled swordfish. We also sauté various white fish, like onaga, opakapaka, and mahimahi. We can satisfy whatever mood you are in. When you come to Longhi's you can expect to have some fantastic seafood, either by itself or with pasta.

IN 1985 MY SON PETER and daughter Carol went to visit their mother in Switzerland. After visiting their mother they went to the Côte d'Azur for several days. They especially enjoyed myriad seafood salads. After leaving this area they went to Florence, Italy. One day while they were walking by the Ponte Vecchio, Peter noticed a delectable-looking salad in the window of a small restaurant. Both agreed after they ate that it was by far the best seafood salad they had ever had. Even though the ones in France were wonderful, this one was superior. Upon returning to the United States, Peter worked on this dish for over a week, using the ingredients that the owner of the small restaurant had told him he used in his terrific salad. I'm happy to say that the results Peter achieved were wonderful, and Frutti di Mare has become one of our most popular dishes.

Frutti di Mare

Bouillon (page 40)

8 ounces squid, cleaned (see page 41)

1 pound scallops

1 pound shrimp, peeled and deveined

$1/4$ cup lemon juice

$1/2$ cup extra virgin olive oil

$1/2$ teaspoon chopped garlic

$1/4$ cup chopped flat-leaf parsley

$1/2$ teaspoon salt

1 teaspoon freshly ground black pepper

$1/4$ cup kalamata olives, pitted and julienned

$1/2$ cup roasted red peppers, seeded, peeled, and julienned

■ In a stockpot over low heat, bring the bouillon to a slow simmer. Add the cleaned squid to the bouillon and poach for 2 to 3 minutes. While the squid is poaching, prepare an ice bath by filling a large bowl with ice and adding just enough water to cover. Drain the squid, shock it in the ice bath, and drain again. Cut the squid into $1/4$-inch rings, leaving the tentacles whole. Poach the scallops in the bouillon for 2 minutes, then shock in the ice bath and drain. Poach the shrimp for 2 minutes in the bouillon, shock in the ice bath, and drain.

■ Combine lemon juice, olive oil, garlic, parsley, salt, and pepper and mix well; add the olives and peppers to the mixture. Toss in the drained seafood, making sure all of it gets well coated. Chill in the refrigerator.

Serves 4

MY FATHER, PAUL LONGHI, affectionately known as PJ, was a great cook. One of his specialties was grilled lobster stuffed with Italian bread crumbs.

At Longhi's we fly in two hundred to four hundred pounds of lobster from Boston each week. After doing much research, Tom White, who does our buying, concluded that the finest lobsters are the Nova Scotia hard shells from the waters above Maine. One of the reasons they are so good is that they come from extremely cold water. The colder the water, the better the lobster.

The Palm restaurant in New York City is famous for their steaks and also for their gigantic lobsters. So with this in mind and thinking about my Dad, I came up with the idea of grilling large lobsters. The only difference we made in my Dad's original recipe was to add chopped macadamia nuts to the bread crumb mixture. I like to use large lobsters for this dish, but you can use smaller ones as well. All you need is a hot grill and some fresh lobsters. Serve this with lemon and melted butter and you will have a wonderfully memorable meal.

Grilled Lobster PJ Style

BREAD CRUMB MIXTURE

1 cup bread crumbs

2 tablespoons finely chopped macadamia nuts

1 stick ($^1/_2$ cup) melted butter

LOBSTER

2 3-pound Maine lobsters

$^1/_2$ stick ($^1/_4$ cup) cold butter, cut into chunks

1 lemon, cut into wedges

■ Preheat broiler or grill. Combine bread crumbs, macadamia nuts, and $^1/_4$ cup of the melted butter in a bowl. Cut each lobster in half lengthwise; crack the claws. Put the lobsters under the broiler or on the grill for 5 minutes. Pull the lobsters out and put the cold butter chunks on the tail, claws, and body; broil 10 more minutes. Take the lobsters out as soon as the shell turns red and the meat becomes opaque. Fill the tails and bodies with the bread crumb mixture. Put lobster back under the broiler or on the grill until brown. Serve with lemon and remaining $^1/_4$ cup melted butter.

Serves 4

ABOUT SHRIMP LONGHI

BEFORE I WENT INTO THE RESTAURANT business I spent many hours cooking. I experimented with different kinds of foods, tried several types of recipes, and worked on developing my culinary creativity. One of these creations was a recipe that I made with bay scallops, the tiny kind that come from Peconic Bay in Long Island, New York. They are difficult to find and have a short season, but if you can find them, they are wonderful. They have a nutty taste and are truly delicious. During my bachelor days this dish was the centerpiece for many of the meals I cooked when entertaining. It was so simple yet so delicious. I knew then that if I ever actually owned a restaurant, this sauce would be one of my most successful creations. The sauce is very simple, made with butter, white wine, lemon, chopped tomato, and fresh basil. Unfortunately, procuring Peconic Bay scallops in Lahaina, Maui, in 1976 proved to be impossible; shrimp, however, were plentiful. So I tried this dish with shrimp, and the sauce complemented them perfectly. I served it over garlic toast and again it was a perfect marriage. Our most famous dish, Shrimp Longhi, was thus created and has been extremely popular for the past twenty years. Other restaurants have asked my permission to serve Shrimp Longhi, and naturally I said yes. If you want to try something great that is not hard to make, try Shrimp Longhi. It's a dish that can be prepared with either shrimp or scallops, or a combination of both. This recipe make enough for two people. If you are making this recipe for four people, use two pans at the same time. Do not attempt to do it all in one pan—the seafood will be crowded and will not cook properly.

Shrimp Longhi

GARLIC TOAST

2 cloves garlic, minced

2 tablespoons butter

2 pieces crusty Italian or French bread

SHRIMP

12 large shrimp (1 pound), rinsed, peeled, and deveined

$1/4$ cup all-purpose flour

3 tablespoons butter

1 tablespoon olive oil

1 cup white wine

1 ounce lemon juice

4 to 6 tablespoons cold butter, cut into chunks

$1/2$ tomato, cut into medium dice

$1/4$ cup chopped basil

■ Preheat broiler. Sauté garlic in butter for 2 or 3 minutes. Dip bread in garlic butter and place under the broiler until lightly browned. Put garlic toast on a serving platter.

■ Dredge shrimp in flour to lightly coat them, shaking off any excess flour. In a sauté pan, combine butter and olive oil over medium heat. When the butter is foamy, add the shrimp to the pan and sauté for 3 to 5 minutes, until shrimp is cooked. Remove shrimp from the pan and pour out any excess butter. Return the pan to medium heat and deglaze with white wine; reduce for 2 to 3 minutes and then add the lemon juice. Reduce liquid by half (approximately 3 minutes). Then stir in 3 tablespoons cold butter chunks. Add more butter to the sauce 1 tablespoon at a time until the sauce becomes emulsified. The sauce should not be thick but just coat the back of a spoon. Add tomato and basil. Return the shrimp to the pan for 30 seconds and toss. Put shrimp on garlic toast and pour sauce over shrimp.

Serves 2

WE SERVE PRAWNS two ways at Longhi's, Prawns Amaretto and Prawns Venice. I created the latter dish several years ago with the idea of having a dish that was strong in garlic and very similar to scampi. (What people call scampi in America is really not scampi in Italy. In Italian scampi is a crustacean—not a flavoring, but the name of an actual creature. In America I will often hear the term Shrimp Scampi, which is a tautology, a repetition of the same thing using different words.) I wanted to create a dish similar to what has become known as Shrimp Scampi, but that would be both different and superior. Another name for this dish is Garlic Shrimp. We use several cloves of garlic in the dish, and it is very strong but the taste is terrific. It can be served as an appetizer or as a main course. Follow the instructions and you will have a grand meal.

Prawns Venice

24 large prawns (2 pounds), unshelled
1/4 cup extra virgin olive oil
1/4 cup finely chopped garlic
1 cup white wine
1/4 cup lemon juice
5 to 6 tablespoons cold butter, cut
    into chunks
1/4 cup chopped flat-leaf parsley

■ Rinse prawns in cool water. Using a sharp knife, without removing the shells, split prawns down the back and remove the vein.

■ Over medium heat, heat half the olive oil in a sauté pan that fits 12 prawns. Sauté the prawns with their shells on for 3 minutes on each side, until done; reserve. Sauté the remaining prawns with the remaining olive oil; reserve. Drain 90 percent of the olive oil from pan. Arrange prawns on four plates. Add chopped garlic to the pan and sauté 1 minute. Add the wine and reduce by half; add the lemon juice and cook 1 minute. Stir 4 tablespoons of the cold butter chunks into sauce at the same time. Stir in more butter if necessary, until sauce emulsifies. Add parsley and remove from heat. Pour sauce over prawns.

Serves 4

WHEN I LIVED IN WASHINGTON, D.C., in the early 70s, Amaretto suddenly became a very popular item. Everybody was talking about it. During this time I was doing a lot of experimenting with cooking and decided I wanted to combine Amaretto in a dish with food. I thought that meat would not go well with Amaretto, fish might be okay—but the best possible marriage that came to mind was prawns. I wanted this dish to be in the Italian style with Asian overtones. I combined Amaretto, orange juice, and cream to enhance the flavor of the prawns.

In 1978 the world-famous artist Guy Buffet collaborated with me on a series of illustrations of four recipes from Longhi's. One of the recipes we picked was Prawns Amaretto. Guy did a fabulous painting of this dish and named it "Two prawns making love under the influence of Amaretto." The *Los Angeles Times* found out about this recipe and wanted to do a feature story on Prawns Amaretto, so I sent them a copy of Buffet's illustration. A few weeks later I opened up the *Los Angeles Times* and on the front page of the food section was a full page story about Prawns Amaretto, featuring the terrific artwork of Guy Buffet and the recipe. That summer we sold more Prawns Amaretto during a three-month period than we had in the first two years of business. Everybody who had read the article came in and wanted to try this dish.

If you like a little sweetness in your food and want to try something different and unique, try this. It's a lot of fun and I know people will enjoy it. It's especially good for an appetizer, but is also terrific as a main course. If you want to double the quantity (say, to serve four as a main course), use two pans at the same time—don't try to make it all in a single pan.

Prawns Amaretto

12 prawns (1 pound), unshelled
3 tablespoons butter
¹/₂ cup brandy
¹/₄ cup white wine
¹/₄ cup orange juice
¹/₃ cup Amaretto
¹/₄ cup heavy cream
¹/₂ teaspoon orange zest

- Rinse prawns in cool water. Using a sharp knife, without removing the shells, split prawns down the back and remove the vein.

- Sauté prawns in butter for about 3 minutes per side until done; reserve. Pour out any excess butter from the pan. Add brandy to the pan and flame the liquid. (Use a match if you do not have a gas stove. Be very careful when flaming alcohol, as the flame ignites very fast and can shoot up quite high.) When the flame goes out, add the white wine and orange juice and reduce by half until syrupy. Add the Amaretto, cream, and orange zest. Simmer for 3 or 4 minutes until it reduces; pour sauce over prawns.

Serves 4 as an appetizer, or 2 as a main course

AHI, A FISH INDIGENOUS TO the Pacific Ocean, is also commonly called yellowfin tuna. Many of our customers at Longhi's asked for ahi, but I was never satisfied with the fact that when we broiled it, it had little excitement and in my opinion was rather blah. (I prefer to eat ahi raw as either sushi or sashimi.) So I decided to create an exciting dish using ahi.

Ahi Torino is a dish that is extremely habit-forming. John McCrea, our manager of Longhi's for the past fifteen years, ate only Ahi Torino for dinner for three years straight. One of our customers, a very famous musical entrepreneur and musician, Jimmy Bowen, eats at Longhi's several times a week. The only main course he ever orders is Ahi Torino, his theory being, "It's so great, why should I try anything else?" Another good thing about this dish is that you don't have to use ahi. You can use any other kind of fish. We do it with mahimahi, with opakapaka, and with onaga. You can use any fish you want. I actually like it best with onaga. It has become one of our great sellers at Longhi's and it's the simplest dish in the world to make. Just remember to get top-quality fish. Marinate it in the refrigerator for several hours—the longer, the better. Cook it quickly, and when you serve it everybody will say you are a great cook.

Ahi Torino

$^1/_2$ cup extra virgin olive oil

2 cloves garlic, chopped

$^1/_4$ cup basil, chopped

2 pounds grade-A, sashimi-quality ahi, cut into 4 half-inch-thick fillets

1 loaf French or Italian bread, or 2 cups bread crumbs

$^1/_4$ cup macadamia nuts, chopped

2 eggs

2 tablespoons butter

1 lemon, cut into 8 pieces

4 tablespoons flat-leaf parsley, chopped

■ Make the marinade by mixing the olive oil, garlic, and basil. Add the ahi and marinate for 2 to 12 hours. Keep refrigerated.

■ Preheat oven to 350°. If you are making your own bread crumbs, cut bread into $1^1/_2$-inch slices and bake in the oven for 15 minutes until golden brown and dry. Place macadamia nuts on a tray and toast in the oven until brown, being careful not to burn. Put bread in a food processor and process until fine. Mix 2 cups bread crumbs with the macadamia nuts.

■ Remove ahi from marinade. Lightly beat eggs. Dip fish in egg and roll in bread crumbs. Pat the bread crumb mixture firmly into the fish, making sure all sides are coated.

■ In a pan over medium heat, add butter; when it foams, add the fish. Do not crowd the pan—cook the fish in two batches if necessary. Cook fish until golden brown on one side; add more butter if needed and turn fish. When the fish is done, squeeze 1 lemon wedge over each piece and remove from the pan. Sprinkle with chopped parsley and serve with a lemon wedge.

Serves 4

OPAKAPAKA IS ONE OF THE MOST delicate fish in Hawaiian waters, and the most sought-after because of its luscious flavor and ability to complement many different sauces and preparations. Red snapper, or any delicate white-fleshed fish, can also be used.

You can vary the sauce by substituting almonds for the grapes. Simply toast ¹/₄ cup slivered almonds or chopped macadamia nuts in a 350° oven for about 10 minutes. Add the nuts to the sauce before serving.

Opakapaka with Grapes

¹/₃ cup flour
2 pounds opakapaka, cut into 4 pieces
3 tablespoons butter
1 tablespoon olive oil
1 cup white wine
1 tablespoon lemon juice
4 to 6 tablespoons cold butter,
    cut into chunks
¹/₄ cup green grapes, halved lengthwise
2 tablespoons chopped flat-leaf parsley

■ Lightly flour fish on both sides. In a sauté pan over medium heat, add 3 tablespoons butter and 1 tablespoon olive oil. When butter foams, add fish to pan. Sauté 3 to 4 minutes on one side and turn; continue cooking 3 to 4 minutes until done. Remove fish from pan; pour out excess butter. Deglaze pan with white wine and lemon juice; reduce liquid by half. Add 3 tablespoons chunked butter; swirl into sauce. Add more cold butter as needed until saucy. Add grapes, then parsley, and pour the sauce over the fish.

Serves 4

MAHIMAHI IS A FIRM, moist, white-fleshed fish that can now be purchased on the mainland as well as in Hawaii. It's perfect for sautéing and holds up beautifully to the opulent taste of roasted macadamia nuts.

Mahimahi with Macadamia Nuts

¹/₄ cup chopped macadamia nuts
¹/₃ cup flour
2 pounds mahimahi, cut into 4 fillets
3 tablespoons plus 1 stick (¹/₂ cup) butter
1 tablespoon olive oil
4 tablespoons lemon juice
2 tablespoons chopped flat-leaf parsley

■ Preheat oven to 350°. Place macadamia nuts in a shallow pan and toast for 5 to 10 minutes until golden brown.

■ Lightly flour fish on both sides. In a sauté pan, melt 3 tablespoons butter and 1 tablespoon olive oil. When pan is hot and butter is foamy, add fish to pan. Sauté 3 to 4 minutes until golden brown; turn fish and continue cooking 2 to 4 minutes until golden brown and done. Remove fish from pan. Add 8 tablespoons butter to pan, simmer until it turns golden brown, then add 4 tablespoons lemon juice. Swirl the pan, then add the macadamia nuts. Shake pan for 20 seconds. Pour the sauce over the fish. Sprinkle fish with chopped parsley.

Serves 4

Meat and Poultry

WHEN WE FIRST OPENED LONGHI'S we did not serve red meat. After one year in operation I was getting such demand from our customers for steaks and lamb chops and veal that I decided to offer a full selection of meat. It has been said over the past two years that one of the best-kept secrets in Hawaii is Longhi's steaks. One of the main reasons for this is Tom White, my roommate at Cornell University and a graduate of its celebrated hotel school. Tom operated three very successful restaurants featuring steaks in Syracuse, New York. In 1979 Tom was voted by the New York Restaurant Association as the Restauranteur of the Year. When Tom came to Longhi's, his job was to make sure we had the best steaks in Hawaii. Tom spent many hours finding out how we could achieve this goal.

It not only takes high-quality meat to make a great steak dinner. You must also know how to treat the steaks and what to serve with them. The steak must be at room temperature when you put it on the grill. I have seen many restaurant cooks mistakenly take a steak directly from the refrigerator and immediately put it on the grill. At Longhi's we marinate our steaks in olive oil, garlic, and basil for four to five hours in the refrigerator, then bring them to room temperature shortly before they are ready to be grilled. If you order your steak rare, it won't be served cold in the middle. Once the steaks are put on the grill, our cooks are experts at cooking them to the proper temperature. Some people like their steaks blood rare, others very well cooked.

On the following pages we will show you a few of the ways we prepare steak at Longhi's. There are many things you can do with a steak besides simply broiling it. At Longhi's we have created many steak variations that have become popular.

When we decided to serve meat, we demanded from our suppliers that they procure for us only the finest products available. All the meat that we use is chilled, never frozen. *Plume de veau* is the best-quality veal on the market. At Longhi's we use the boneless veal strip loins of this quality for the scallopini dishes. This white veal comes from an extremely young animal and is very tender. We have a contract with a wonderful poultry company in Honolulu that flies fresh chicken to us several times during the week.

WHEN I LIVED IN NEW YORK CITY in the early 60s there was a section of Manhattan commonly referred to as Steak Row. These restaurants were on 45th and 46th streets between Second Avenue and Lexington, and were primarily run by Italians. (Many people don't realize that some of the world's finest steaks are found in Italy, especially in Tuscany.) Most of these New York restaurants still exist and still serve fabulous steaks. I particularly remember the Palm on Second Avenue, The Pen and Pencil, Pietro's, Christ Cella, and The Press Box. These restaurants were owned by men with such fabulous names as Bozzi and Ganzi, Bruno and Manfredi. As I am an Italian these names are especially appealing to me, evoking memories of time spent in Tuscany enjoying some of the most sublime steak feasts imaginable—such as the famous *bistecca alla fiorentina*, which according to Tuscan tradition must come only from Chianina steer.

These New York restaurants had a unique way of serving their steaks. After broiling them to perfection they would splash fresh butter over the steaks immediately before serving them. I thought this was a great idea, so when we started serving steaks at Longhi's I wanted to do this. But I also felt I could create an even more exciting way of serving steaks by adding basil to the butter, making it even more tantalizing. After much thought I came up with the original title for this great steak creation: Steak Longhi.

Steak Longhi

MARINADE
³/₄ cup extra virgin olive oil
2 or 3 cloves garlic, minced
4 basil leaves, chopped

STEAK
4 New York strip steaks, 1¹/₂ inches thick
1 stick (¹/₂ cup) salted butter
¹/₂ cup chopped basil

■ In a large shallow glass dish, make the marinade by combining the olive oil, garlic, and chopped basil leaves. Immerse the meat and let it marinate 4 to 24 hours in the refrigerator. Remove meat from refrigerator at least 30 minutes before cooking.

■ At Longhi's we grill our steaks. You can grill the steaks, broil them, or panfry them in a cast-iron pan. Whichever you choose, make sure the cooking surface is hot before you put the steaks on. Cook 4 to 6 minutes per side for rare, 8 minutes for medium rare, and 10 to 12 minutes per side for well done. When the steaks are cooked to the desired temperature, remove them from the heat.

■ Melt the butter in a saucepan over medium heat. Add chopped basil and cook for 30 seconds; remove from heat. Cut steaks on the bias into ¹/₄-inch slices and fan out on serving plates. Pour sauce over steak and serve.

Serves 4

AS I MENTIONED EARLIER, the Palm in New York City is one of my favorite restaurants. They have a dish they call Steak à la Palm. The steak is cut into strips on the bias and laid over a bed of garlic toast, roasted mancini peppers, and grilled onions. The waiters at the Palm served as an inspiration to me in my creation of the verbal menu. Although they had many other items on the menu, their standard question was, "Do you want steak or lobster?" If you asked for anything else, they would say in a shocked manner, "What's the matter? Don't you like steak or lobster?" and reluctantly take your order for one of their other items. If you asked for a menu, the standard retort was, "Did you come here to eat or did you come here to read? If you want to read, the biggest library in the world is just down the street. If you have come to eat, just leave it up to me and I'll take care of you."

Steak à la Palm

MARINADE

$3/4$ cup extra virgin olive oil

2 or 3 cloves garlic, minced

4 basil leaves, chopped

STEAK

4 New York strip steaks, $1^1/_2$ inches thick

2 tablespoons butter

2 tablespoons olive oil

1 onion, thinly sliced

1 cup mancini peppers, julienned

4 pieces garlic toast

- In a large shallow glass dish, make the marinade by combining the olive oil, garlic, and chopped basil leaves. Immerse the meat and let it marinate 4 to 24 hours in the refrigerator. Remove meat from refrigerator at least 30 minutes before cooking.

- Heat butter and oil in a saucepan over low to medium heat. Add the sliced onion, let cook about 10 minutes, then add the peppers; continue cooking until the onions caramelize. While onions and peppers are cooking, start the steaks.

- When the grill is hot, put steaks on, cooking 4 to 6 minutes per side for rare, 8 minutes for medium rare, and 10 to 12 minutes per side for well done. When steaks are cooked to desired temperature, remove them from the grill.

- Cut the steaks on the bias into $1/_4$-inch slices and fan out on top of the garlic toast. Top with onions and peppers and serve.

Serves 4

I FEEL THAT A GRILLED FILET MIGNON served in the classic style is rather boring and doesn't have much visual appeal. Even though it is wonderful to eat, it could be improved upon, so I created Filet Longhi. The addition of red and yellow peppers enhanced by the flavors of garlic and anchovy gives the beef a unique and exciting taste. Apparently this combination works, because it has become our number-one seller in the steak category.

Filet Longhi

4 filets mignon, $^1/_2$ to 2 inches thick

3 tablespoons extra virgin olive oil

2 cloves garlic, chopped

1 oil-packed anchovy, rinsed in water
   and minced

1 red bell pepper, cut into $^1/_4$-inch strips

1 yellow bell pepper, cut into thin
   $^1/_4$-inch strips

1 stick ($^1/_2$ cup) salted butter

$^1/_2$ cup chopped basil

■ Remove the beef from refrigerator at least 30 minutes before cooking. When the grill is hot, put on the filets. While they're cooking, add olive oil to a sauté pan and sauté the garlic for 30 seconds. Add the minced anchovy and then the peppers; sauté until the peppers are soft. Turn the filets only once while cooking.

■ When the steaks are cooked to the desired temperature, take them off the grill. Melt the butter in a saucepan over medium heat. When butter is foamy, add chopped basil and cook for 30 seconds. Remove from heat.

■ Cut the filets on the bias into $^1/_4$-inch slices and fan out on 4 individual plates. Pour sauce over steaks. Place sautéed peppers to the side of the steak.

Serves 4

SEND IT BACK!

If you get a steak at Longhi's that doesn't satisfy you, we will gladly prepare another one for you. (If you are not happy with your meal at Longhi's, you don't have to pay because we don't want anybody walking out of Longhi's who did not feel they got their money's worth. If I get a letter of complaint, which does happen in this business, I give them a refund.)

WHEN LONGHI'S WAS in its infant stages, a friend of mine, Sal Greco, whose name means Greek in Italian, worked for me for a short time. Sal was my host and, more importantly, a good personal friend. Sal's family was from the southern part of Italy called Calabria. Sal kept telling me about a dish that his grandmother made. After importuning me for several days to try this recipe, I decided to do so. The dish is very simple: we add Marsala and anchovies to our basic Pomodoro Sauce. This combination works beautifully and synergizes extremely well. This sauce, which we have used at Longhi's for twenty years, can be used on many things, such as pasta, chicken, or veal. Thank you, Sal, for your contribution. We love it.

Chicken Mediterranean

4 boneless, skinless chicken breasts

2 eggs

$1/4$ cup flour

$3/4$ cup grated Parmesan cheese

$3/4$ cup olive oil

2 oil-packed anchovies, chopped

2 cloves garlic, chopped

$1/2$ teaspoon crushed red pepper flakes

$1/2$ tomato, chopped (about $1/2$ cup)

1 ounce sweet Marsala

1 ounce dry Marsala

$1/4$ cup chopped basil

$1 1/2$ cups Pomodoro Sauce (page 23)

■ Pound the chicken breasts and coat with egg, flour, and cheese as described in the recipe for Chicken Parmesan (page 72).

■ Heat $1/2$ cup of the olive oil in a cast-iron skillet. Panfry the chicken (two pieces at a time, if the pan is small) over medium heat until golden brown. Turn pieces over and brown the other side. Remove chicken from pan.

■ Add the remaining $1/4$ cup of olive oil to a clean sauté pan and sauté the chopped anchovies for 30 seconds. Add the garlic and crushed red pepper flakes. Then add the chopped tomato and sauté for 3 minutes. Add the wine and let reduce for 3 minutes, then add chopped basil. Add Pomodoro Sauce and mix well. Pour sauce over chicken and serve.

Serves 4

FOR THE THREE YEARS PRIOR to opening Longhi's I was a vegetarian. When I opened Longhi's I felt it would be appropriate to expand the menu, not only because it would be economically beneficial but also to offer my customers a wide variety of choices. While I continued to eschew red meat, I did serve chicken and fish, using chicken instead of veal.

When I opened Longhi's we had chicken Parmesan, we had chicken piccata, we had chicken Marsala, and we prepared it in other ways. Not only is chicken less expensive than veal, but it also gives a better result. I was so confident that chicken breasts, if prepared properly, would be as good as veal, if not better, that I ran an advertisement with my friend Arnawood Iskenderian. We used to do a radio show, and Arnawood would say, "I hate chicken. At least I used to hate chicken until I went to Longhi's last night, and Bob asked me to try his veal Parmesan. After I ate it, I said 'This is fantastic, this is the best veal Parmesan I ever had in my life.'" To which I replied, "Arnawood, that wasn't veal, that was chicken." We then ended the program by saying, "If you want to have the best chicken you've ever had in your life, come to Longhi's and try our chicken Parmesan."

This is another dish that seems to be addictive. Two of my customers—Doug Hajjar, an entrepreneur and computer genius, and his wife Mary—travel 35 miles three or four times a week to dine at Longhi's. Doug and Mary always have the same main course, and that is chicken Parmesan. I have been trying for years to convince them to order some of our other great dishes, but their theory again, like Jimmy Bowen's, is "We like it so much, why should we change?"

When making this dish, only use fresh chicken. You do not need to use Parmigiano-Reggiano; good domestic Parmesan will do just as well.

Chicken Parmesan

2 cups Pomodoro Sauce (page 23)
4 boneless, skinless chicken breasts
$^1/_4$ cup flour
$^3/_4$ cup plus 3 tablespoons grated Parmesan cheese
2 eggs
$^1/_2$ cup olive oil
4 slices mozzarella
4 tablespoons chopped flat-leaf parsley

■ Prepare Pomodoro Sauce and keep warm.

■ Pound each chicken breast with a meat mallet between two pieces of wax paper or plastic wrap to an even $^1/_3$-inch thickness. Preheat oven broiler. Combine the flour and $^3/_4$ cup grated Parmesan in a shallow bowl. Lightly beat the eggs in another bowl. Dip each chicken breast in the beaten eggs, then bread with the flour and cheese mixture.

■ Heat the olive a oil in cast-iron skillet. When the oil is hot, panfry the chicken (two pieces at a time, if the pan is small) over medium heat until golden brown. Turn the pieces over and brown the other side. Drain the chicken on paper towels. Put the chicken on a flat broiler pan and top with mozzarella; place under the broiler until the cheese melts. Remove from the oven, top with Pomodoro Sauce, and sprinkle with Parmesan and chopped flat-leaf parsley.

Serves 4

This dish can also be served with a simple caper sauce, such as the one that follows.

Chicken Piccata Longhi Style

4 boneless, skinless chicken breasts

2 eggs

$1/4$ cup flour

$3/4$ cup grated Parmesan cheese

$1/2$ cup olive oil

Juice of 1 lemon

- Pound the chicken breasts and coat with egg, flour, and cheese as described in the recipe for Chicken Parmesan (see opposite page).

- Heat the olive oil in a cast-iron skillet, then panfry the chicken (2 pieces at a time, if the pan is small) over medium heat until golden brown. Turn pieces over and brown the other side. Squeeze lemon juice over chicken and serve.

LEMON, BUTTER, AND CAPER SAUCE

1 cup white wine

3 ounces lemon juice

5 tablespoons cold butter, cut into chunks

$1/4$ cup capers

- After the chicken is cooked, remove it from the pan and drain off any excess juices and/or fat. Add the wine to the pan and reduce for 1 minute. Add the lemon juice and let simmer a few minutes to reduce by half. Stir the cold butter into the sauce, starting with 3 tablespoons and adding more as the butter is absorbed into the sauce. Add capers and stir until saucy. Pour sauce over chicken.

Serves 4

USE 1-INCH-THICK LOIN veal chops weighing 10 to 12 ounces. Do not overcook veal chops, and be aware that veal cooks much more quickly than beef.

Veal Chops with Porcini Mushrooms

3 ounces dried porcini, rehydrated in
    warm water, or 2 cups fresh porcini,
    sliced
4 veal chops, 1 inch thick
Salt
Freshly ground black pepper
2 tablespoons butter, at room
    temperature
$^1/_2$ medium onion, thinly sliced
$^1/_4$ cup white wine
$^1/_2$ cup sweet Marsala
$^1/_2$ cup dry Marsala
$^1/_4$ cup lemon juice
2 tablespoons porcini soaking
    water (if using dried)
6 tablespoons cold butter, cut into chunks
$^1/_4$ cup fresh chopped basil

■ Cover dried porcini with warm water and let soak for 15 minutes, until soft. Drain, reserving 1 ounce of the soaking water.

■ Salt and pepper the veal chops. Prepare grill or preheat broiler. Cook 4 to 6 minutes on each side for medium rare.

■ In a sauté pan over medium heat, melt 2 tablespoons butter; add the sliced onions and cook for 3 minutes until soft. Turn up the heat and add the white wine, then the sweet and dry Marsala. After 30 seconds add the lemon juice and porcini soaking water. Let the sauce reduce for approximately 5 minutes. Mix 3 tablespoons cold chunked butter into sauce. Add porcini and 3 more tablespoons cold butter to the pan, stirring until sauce thickens. (If using fresh porcini mushrooms, cook a few minutes until mushrooms are soft before adding final butter.) Add basil. Pour the sauce over the veal chops.

■ This sauce can be prepared as you are grilling or just before you cook the veal chops.

Serves 4

VEAL SCALLOPINI IS EXCELLENT for sautéing because it is so thin. The pounding tenderizes the meat so that it can be cooked very quickly. Just remember, do not crowd the pan with too much veal or the meat will steam. It is better to sauté the veal in batches.

Veal Marsala

$^1/_4$ **cup flour**

8 pieces (about 1$^1/_2$ pounds scallopini veal, pounded thin

6 tablespoons butter, at room temperature

2 tablespoons olive oil

$^1/_4$ **cup white wine**

$^1/_2$ **cup sweet Marsala**

$^1/_2$ **cup dry Marsala**

1 tablespoon lemon juice

5 to 6 tablespoons cold butter, cut into chunks

2 cups sliced mushrooms

$^1/_4$ **cup chopped fresh basil**

■ Lightly flour the veal. In a sauté pan over medium heat, melt 3 tablespoons of the room-temperature butter and 1 tablespoon olive oil until foam subsides. Add 4 pieces of the veal to the pan; sauté 2 minutes on each side, until done. Pour off any remaining butter, put pan back on the heat, and add the remaining 3 tablespoons butter and 1 tablespoon olive oil; sauté the remaining veal. Remove veal from the pan and pour off any remaining butter. Add the white wine to the pan and simmer 30 seconds. Add the Marsala and reduce by half. Add the lemon juice, then stir 5 to 6 tablespoons of cold butter chunks into the sauce. When the butter has melted, add the sliced mushrooms. Simmer until the mushrooms are cooked, about 1 minute. Finish sauce by adding chopped basil. Pour sauce over veal and serve.

Serves 4

Veal Piccata

1/3 cup flour

8 pieces (about 1 1/2 pounds) scallopini
    veal, pounded thin

6 tablespoons butter, at room
    temperature

2 tablespoons olive oil

1 cup white wine

1/3 cup lemon juice

5 to 6 tablespoons cold butter,
    cut into chunks

1/4 cup capers

1/4 cup chopped parsley

■ Lightly flour the veal. Heat 3 tablespoons butter and 1 tablespoon olive oil in a sauté pan over medium heat. Add 4 pieces of veal. (Do not crowd the pan or the veal will steam! It is better to sauté veal in two batches.) Sauté veal for 2 minutes on each side until done; remove from pan. Pour off any remaining butter, put pan back on the heat, and add the remaining 3 tablespoons butter and 1 tablespoon olive oil; sauté the remaining veal. Remove veal from the pan and pour off any remaining butter.

■ Return the pan to the stove over medium heat. Deglaze the pan by adding the wine and reduce 1 minute. Add lemon juice, cooking 2 to 3 minutes to reduce liquid by half. Add 5 to 6 tablespoons of cold butter chunks to the pan. Swirl the butter into the reduced liquid; the sauce will emulsify. Add the capers. Place two pieces of veal on each plate and pour the sauce over. Finally, sprinkle with chopped parsley.

Serves 4

Sandwiches, Vegetables, and Salads

I HAVE MENTIONED SEVERAL TIMES that when I opened Longhi's I was a vegetarian. In the '70s, although some ethnic restaurants served excellent fresh vegetables, most other establishments served them frozen and certainly did not put much thought into their preparation. I am glad to say that eating fresh vegetables has become much more popular in America, and most eateries serve them with style.

At Longhi's we feel that vegetables are an extremely important part of the meal, so we always have myriad vegetable dishes available. We serve the majestic asparagus, the stately artichoke, beautiful eggplant and zucchini, various types of mushrooms, succulent peas (both the English and the sugar snap varieties), red and yellow peppers (I prefer them to the green), and healthy spinach, green beans, broccoli, and cauliflower. Everything is à la carte at Longhi's, so that each dish is separately served. This is the way the Italians eat and the way that I prefer to dine. By serving the food in this manner, your plate is not crowded with several different kinds of food, which in my opinion diminishes the taste of each individual item. We can offer you a beautiful plate of fresh peas, zucchini fritta, artichoke Longhi, asparagus Parmesan, spinach sautéed with garlic, or a filling dish such as eggplant Parmesan. When you eat at Longhi's, make sure you take advantage of our wonderful vegetables. They not only are great for your health but will enhance your meal.

An old French truism says it takes three things to make a great salad. First, you must be a spendthrift with the olive oil. Second, you must be a miser with the vinegar. And third, you must be a madman with the tossing. If you apply these three principles when making salads, you will be a superb salad maker.

In addition, you need a good wooden salad bowl. Never wash it with soap and water. After each use keep the bowl clean by wiping it out with a paper towel. This will enable the bowl to absorb the oil and eventually become perfectly seasoned. Also made of wood are the two large wooden spoons I use, which enable me to conform to the third principle of salad making by mixing the salad like a madman.

I prefer to use cold pressed extra virgin olive oil. It is the most expensive, but it is also the best, and in spite of its high price it is the only kind of olive oil we use for salads at Longhi's. Fortunately, in the past decade health experts have come to the conclusion that olive oil is the best oil for your well-being.

You can use different kinds of vinegar. I prefer red wine vinegar. Balsamic vinegar is very popular but also very powerful; it changes the relationship of the olive oil, so you must use much less. You can combine a small amount of balsamic with the red wine vinegar to produce an excellent result.

One of the best things about making salads is that you can use the full gamut of ingredients to create your own dressings. Fresh herbs can be used, as can Dijon mustard or different kinds of cheese, such as feta or Gorgonzola. Always put the vinegar in the bowl first,

then add salt and pepper, the Dijon mustard, the herbs, and (if you are using it) add the cheese last. It is very important that all the ingredients you use be mixed with the vinegar before you add the olive oil. The proper proportion in most dressings is three parts olive oil to one part vinegar. If you mix the salad dressing in the bowl, you can add the lettuce and other vegetables to the bowl and mix the salad immediately. Another thing to remember is to clean the lettuce in cold water, then dry the leaves in a salad spinner, wrap them in paper towels and put them in the refrigerator for at least an hour. Your greens will be crisp and fresh-tasting, and you will get the maximum results from your salad.

Just remember that salads are not difficult. Many people are fearful of salads because they feel that they do not know how to make them properly. They have been using bottled dressings found in the supermarket. I personally do not like prepared salad dressings. At Longhi's we use freshly made salad dressings, and our customers have lauded our salads for twenty years. If you follow these instructions, you too can gain a reputation for originality in salad making.

Longhi's offers a large lunch menu, and the extensive dinner menu is also available at lunch in smaller portions priced accordingly. The sandwiches in this chapter have proven to be very popular and are a selection of my favorites.

Grilled Chicken Sandwich

MARINADE

$^1/_2$ cup olive oil

2 cloves garlic, chopped

$^1/_4$ teaspoon crushed red pepper flakes

2 tablespoons chopped ginger

2 tablespoons chopped cilantro

Juice of 2 limes

4 boneless, skinless chicken breasts

2 tablespoons salted butter

1 sweet onion, thinly sliced

4 sandwich rolls or buns

■ Combine olive oil with garlic, pepper flakes, ginger, cilantro, and lime juice. Pound chicken breasts lightly until an even thickness is achieved, and marinate in the refrigerator for 2 to 6 hours.

■ In a sauté pan over low heat, heat the butter until foamy. Add the onions and cook uncovered for 15 to 20 minutes, until onions are golden brown and caramelized.

■ Prepare the grill. When it is hot, grill the chicken for 6 to 8 minutes until done. Place chicken on rolls or buns, top with caramelized onions, and serve.

Serves 4

Steak Sandwich Bob Style

MARINADE

$^3/_4$ cup olive oil

2 or 3 cloves garlic, minced

4 chopped basil leaves

4 New York strip steaks, 6 to 8 ounces each

2 tablespoons salted butter

1 tablespoon olive oil

1 sweet onion, sliced

1 teaspoon brown sugar (optional)

1 cup mancini peppers, julienned

4 hoagie rolls or other good bread

Salt and pepper

■ In a large shallow glass dish, make the marinade by combining the olive oil, garlic, and basil. Immerse the meat and let marinate in the refrigerator for 4 to 24 hours. Remove at least 30 minutes before cooking.

■ In a sauté pan over medium heat, melt the butter with the olive oil. Add the onions and lower heat; cook uncovered until onions caramelize, about 15 to 20 minutes, or add brown sugar and cook for 5 minutes. Add the peppers and sauté 30 seconds.

■ Grill, broil, or panfry the steaks in a cast-iron pan while onions cook.

■ Remove the steaks from the heat and finish the onion and peppers. Slice the steaks on the bias; place slices on the hoagie rolls and top with onions and peppers. Season with salt and pepper.

Serves 4

IN THE EARLY 60s, when I lived in New York City, I especially enjoyed dining in a section of downtown Manhattan called Little Italy, which had some fantastic restaurants serving mostly southern Italian cuisine. One of my favorites was the Grotta Azzurra. They always had a line and a wait of up to an hour. The owner would not accept credit cards, personal checks, or lira; only cash! One of the great dishes they had was called Spedini. Spedini is bread with mozzarella cheese, deep-fried and topped with a tomato sauce or an anchovy-butter sauce. I decided that instead of serving it as an appetizer, as it was served at the Grotta, I would serve it as a sandwich for lunch. We did many experiments with this dish. All of my children came up with a different rendition of it. After much bickering, we decided that my youngest son Charlie's version was the best. Again this dish is simple to make: you must use top-quality mozzarella and good Italian or French bread. After the sandwich has been fried in the olive oil, top it with tomato sauce or anchovy butter (which is the way I prefer it). Give it a try—I know you will love it.

Spedini

$^1/_2$ **pound sliced mozzarella cheese**

8 slices of 1-inch -thick crusty Italian bread

4 eggs

Olive oil

4 cups Pomodoro Sauce (page 23)

$^1/_4$ **cup grated Parmesan cheese**

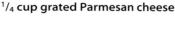

■ Put cheese slices between bread slices to make four sandwiches; press bread down firmly with hands to flatten. Beat the eggs in a bowl. Dip the sandwiches in the egg batter. Heat 1 inch of olive oil in a cast-iron skillet over medium heat. Fry sandwiches on one side; turn when golden brown, and cook other side. Transfer to paper towels to drain. Smother sandwiches with hot Pomodoro Sauce and sprinkle with Parmesan cheese.

Serves 4

Variations:

Copa Spedini

■ Add slice of copacolla ham to sandwich before frying.

Spedini with Anchovy Butter

■ Make spedini as instructed above, but top with anchovy butter instead of Pomodoro Sauce.

Anchovy butter

4 anchovies, rinsed in water and minced

1 stick ($^1/_2$ cup) butter

■ Melt the butter until foamy; add anchovies and sauté 30 seconds.

MY FAVORITE CUISINE (besides Italian) is Chinese. It has been said that there are three great cuisines in the world: French, Italian, and Chinese. I believe if one considers everything, it's pretty hard to beat the Chinese. They have the most varied cuisine in the world, ranging from the food of Canton (which is primarily seafood and rice) to the cuisine of Beijing (which is much more meat- and wheat-oriented). In addition, they have many other styles of cooking, such as Szechwan, which is very hot; Shanghai, which is more oily; and many others that I am not familiar with.

One of my favorite dishes in the world is Peking Duck. In Washington, D.C., there was a restaurant called the Peking Restaurant. It was one of the first northern Chinese restaurants in America. In the 1960s our family would go to the Peking Restaurant every Sunday, and the owner would conjure up a feast. These meals were great culinary experiences. One of the featured items was Peking Duck, and I fell madly in love with it after my first bite. Anytime I could find Peking Duck, I would order it.

After I opened Longhi's and was thinking of different sandwiches I could put on the lunch menu, it occurred to me: Why not make a Peking Duck sandwich? I realize that classic Peking Duck should be hung for several hours, that the skin is eaten first, and that there is a ritual to serving it. But I also knew that the result would not be too much different if we roasted fresh duck, added hoisin sauce and some fresh scallions, and served it in a bun similar to the ones that many Chinese restaurants use. When I opened my delicatessen the featured sandwich was Peking Duck. It was so popular, I decided to put it on the lunch menu at Longhi's. This dish is a lot of fun to serve, and people will be wowed when they eat it.

Peking Duck Sandwich

3-pound duck
Salt and pepper
4 soft hoagie rolls
4 scallions
Hoisin sauce

■ Preheat oven to 375°. Score duck skin with a knife and season with salt and pepper. Roast in oven until cooked, about an hour. (Use a meat thermometer to test the duck; the internal temperature should reach 160°.) When the duck is cool enough to handle, pull the meat from the bones. Warm the rolls in the oven. Chop the green part of the scallions into $1/2$-inch lengths. When the rolls are warm, remove them from the oven, slice, and spread with hoisin sauce. Add a generous amount of duck to each sandwich and sprinkle with the scallions.

Serves 4

UNTIL RECENTLY, MOST ARTICHOKES were eaten by Italians or other ethnic groups, such as Greeks, Spaniards, and other Mediterranean people. Most Americans had never heard of artichokes, and they probably had never eaten them.

It so happens that almost all the artichokes grown in America come from Castroville, California. Every year since the 1950s, Castroville has hosted a large artichoke festival that lasts several days. (The first Miss Artichoke was none other than Marilyn Monroe.) They serve artichokes in a multitude of ways, but they don't serve them Longhi-style. We have been serving artichokes since we opened, and it's by far one of our best sellers. We serve it as an appetizer, as an accompaniment to a meal, or even as a main course. We have been very fortunate that the family of a friend of mine, Mike Jost, owns an artichoke farm in California's Salinas Valley. He consistently supplies us with the finest, largest, and freshest globe artichokes that one can possibly find.

Artichokes are one vegetable that are not good cooked al dente. You do not want them hard; they must be cooked so that the heart (some people call it the bottom) is soft. For this recipe, you must use Parmigiano-Reggiano cheese if you want the best result. Use the best ingredients and you will have a dish you will love.

Artichoke Longhi

4 large globe artichokes
$1/2$ cup grated Parmigiano-Reggiano
Juice of 1 lemon
2 sticks (1 cup) butter

■ To prepare the artichokes, cut off their stems and remove the tough outer leaves with scissors. Cut off the top inch of each artichoke.

■ Steam or boil the artichokes for 20 minutes, until the heart is tender when pierced with a fork. Remove the artichokes from the steamer or cooking vessel. Spread the leaves on top, then reach in and grab the inner pointy leaves and pull these out. Underneath this you will see the hairs of the artichoke; directly underneath these are the heart. Carefully spoon out the hairs but do not go too deep into the heart. You can prepare the artichokes up to 6 hours in advance, reheating them in boiling water or a steamer.

■ Sprinkle each hot artichoke with Parmesan. In a small saucepan bring lemon juice to a boil; add chunks of cold butter and stir constantly so the sauce doesn't break. When the butter is fully melted, pour it over the artichokes.

Serves 4

EGGPLANT, LIKE ARTICHOKE, is another vegetable many Americans never used to eat. Most of the Mediterranean countries have utilized both of these vegetables in many of their dishes, but most Americans have shunned eggplant throughout their life. When people tell me they hate eggplant, I ask if they've ever had it, and they say, "No, I never had it—but I know I won't like it." I believe that eggplant is one of the most wonderful foods in the world, and it is my favorite vegetable. We have been cooking eggplant at Longhi's since we opened.

Whenever I read about eggplant in cookbooks, they say you must slice the eggplant, salt it, and drain it in a colander for an hour. I can say that I have eaten as much eggplant as anyone on this planet, and my restaurant has served tons of it, and I have never salted eggplant either in my restaurant or in my home cooking. My friends who cook eggplant also have never done it and still get wonderful results. My friends who did try salting the eggplant thought that it considerably diminished the taste. Eggplant does not need to be salted and it does not have to be drained. You can cut it and use it right away. Salting the eggplant just seems to make the eggplant salty.

The secret to this dish is adding Parmesan cheese to the flour. Adding the Parmesan gives the dish a regal flavor most versions do not have. We use the best mozzarella cheese when we make our eggplant Parmesan. Twenty years ago I started flying in mozzarella from New York City. I am a firm believer that the mozzarella on the East Coast is far superior to West Coast mozzarella. I like a brand called Polly-O, which is the most popular brand in America. We had a slogan at one time that stated, "We spend more money to fly it than we do to buy it." Although that wasn't quite true, it was pretty close.

Eggplant Parmesan

2 medium eggplant

3 eggs

$^1/_2$ cup flour

$1^1/_2$ cups grated Parmesan cheese

Olive oil

8 slices mozzarella cheese

4 cups Pomodoro Sauce (see page 23)

4 teaspoons Parmigiano-Reggiano
   Parmesan cheese, grated for garnish

- Slice eggplant at a crosswise angle into $^1/_2$-inch slices. Lightly beat eggs in a glass bowl large enough to immerse the eggplant slices. Combine the flour and grated cheese in another bowl. Dip the eggplant slices in the beaten egg, then bread the slices in the flour and cheese mixture, making sure all sides are coated.

- Heat enough olive oil in a heavy skillet over medium heat to halfway cover the eggplant slices. Add the eggplant slices and panfry until golden brown on the bottom, then flip them and brown the other side. When eggplant is cooked, drain slices on paper towels.

- Place cooked eggplant slices on a metal tray and top each with a slice of mozzarella cheese. Place tray under a preheated broiler until the cheese melts. Place two eggplant slices on each plate and cover with heated Pomodoro Sauce. Top with a sprinkle of Parmigiano-Reggiano.

Serves 4

Eggplant Parmesan Variation

▨ Another way to make this dish is to bake it in a 400° oven for 10 to 15 minutes, until the cheese is melted and the eggplant is hot. Line the bottom of a baking dish with a layer of eggplant, topping it with mozzarella cheese and Pomodoro Sauce. You can repeat with another layer of eggplant, cheese, and tomato sauce if you wish. Bake as directed above.

REFRESH THE CRISPY zucchini with a squeeze of lemon to cut the richness of the Parmesan cheese crust.

Zucchini Fritta

4 medium zucchini

3 eggs

1 1/2 cups grated Parmesan cheese

1/2 cup flour

1/2 to 3/4 cup olive oil

Salt

1 lemon

▨ Cut zucchini into long strips. Lightly beat the eggs and set aside in a shallow glass bowl. Combine the grated cheese and flour in a separate bowl. Coat the zucchini strips with egg, then roll them in the flour and cheese mixture, coating all sides. Heat olive oil in a heavy pan; add the zucchini strips, turning when brown. When all sides are brown, drain on paper towels. Continue cooking until all the zucchini are done, adding more oil as needed.

▨ Place zucchini strips on a plate, add salt to taste and squeeze lemon juice over them.

Serves 4

ABOUT ASPARAGUS PARMESAN

WHEN I FIRST CAME TO MAUI, one of the local restauranteurs looked at my menu and was astounded that I would be serving fresh asparagus. For some reason he thought that the expense would be prohibitive and that people would not pay to have fresh asparagus. In my opinion the only way to eat asparagus is fresh, and any other way is just a waste of time. We are fortunate to know a farmer who grows wonderful asparagus for us on the slopes of Haleakala.

At Longhi's we serve asparagus in the classic method used in Ravenna, Italy. Nineteen hundred years ago Martial wrote that Ravenna produced the best asparagus in Italy. Nineteen centuries later, the cognoscenti of asparagus lovers still consider Ravenna their mecca. We serve asparagus very simply—steaming it and adding Parmesan cheese and butter. This dish can be made with browned, burnt, or regular butter but remember to use Parmigiano-Reggiano cheese. This is a very important ingredient in bringing this dish to the heights that it deserves.

Asparagus Parmesan

1 pound asparagus

¹/₃ cup grated Parmigiano-Reggiano cheese

¹/₂ stick (¹/₄ cup) salted butter

≈

 Wash asparagus and cut off tough ends. Steam asparagus for 4 or 5 minutes, or until it is cooked but crisp. Do not overcook. When asparagus is done, drain and set aside on a platter. Sprinkle with the cheese.

In a large saucepan over medium heat, melt the butter and continue cooking until it turns golden brown. When the butter is very brown but not burned, pour it over the cooked asparagus.

Serves 4

THIS CLASSIC PREPARATION is excellent served with fish, chicken, or veal.

Sautéed Spinach in Olive Oil and Parmesan

1 pound fresh spinach, washed

3 cloves garlic, chopped

¹/₂ cup extra virgin olive oil

¹/₂ cup grated Parmigiano-Reggiano cheese

≈

 Wash spinach well, making sure all dirt and sand is removed. Soaking the leaves in water for 20 minutes helps rid them of the sandy grit that seems to stick to fresh spinach. In a large flat pan over medium heat, sauté the garlic in olive oil for about 30 seconds; do not let it burn. Add the spinach to the pan and toss until it wilts. The volume of spinach will shrink considerably. Toss in the Parmesan cheese. Serve.

Serves 4

BREAKFAST AT LONGHI'S has become a tradition. There are several reasons for this. Randy Ortega and his staff bake outrageous pastries every morning. We have a large menu selection, ranging from waffles to smoked salmon. The third reason is the Italian omelets we feature called frittatas. Italians eat frittatas for lunch or as a light dinner. They are easy to prepare, and one of the great things about frittatas is that many different ingredients can be used when making them. They are basically an egg omelet that can either be baked in the oven or slowly cooked on top of the stove. Unlike a French omelet, which cooks in a few minutes, a frittata can bake as long as an hour in the oven or as short as 10 minutes on top of the stove. Frittatas offer a wonderful opportunity to use creativity and imagination when cooking. A wide variety of vegetables can be used as well as an assortment of cheeses. I especially like fresh ricotta, as I feel it gives the frittata a terrific creamy consistency and a fabulous texture. You can also add seafood, meat, or just about anything you want.

Zucchini Frittata with Onions, Mushrooms, and Basil

1 cup sliced onion

$^1/_4$ cup olive oil

2 medium zucchini, cut into $^1/_4$-inch rounds and quartered

2 cups sliced mushrooms

$^1/_4$ teaspoon salt

6 eggs

$^3/_4$ cup grated Parmigiano-Reggiano cheese

$^1/_4$ cup ricotta cheese

12 basil leaves, coarsely chopped

7 twists freshly ground pepper

2 tablespoons butter

■ Sauté onion in olive oil until golden brown. Add the zucchini, mushrooms, and salt. Sauté until cooked. Pour off oil and remove vegetables from pan with a slotted spoon. Allow vegetables to cool.

■ In a bowl, beat the eggs until yolks and whites are combined. Add the Parmesan and ricotta cheeses to the egg mixture, then mix in the vegetables, basil, and pepper.

■ Melt the butter in a 10-inch cast-iron skillet. Do not let it brown. Add the egg mixture and turn the heat down very low. Cook 15 minutes, until eggs have set and thickened and only the top surface is runny. Put the skillet under the broiler for 30 to 60 seconds, until the top is set. Loosen frittata from pan and cut into four wedges. Serve with focaccia or crusty Italian bread.

Serves 4

WHEN I USED TO DINE in New York City there was a restauranteur named Romeo Salta who used cannellini beans in some of his salads. I always thought this was a great idea and wanted to have a salad on my menu that had cannellini beans in it. With this in mind I created Longhi Salad, which has been on the menu since we opened. Guy Buffet did an illustrated recipe of it, and it has become our most popular salad.

This salad also incorporates fresh, crisp green beans, which contrast nicely with the soft cannellini beans. Use domestic Gorgonzola for this salad; Italian Gorgonzola is extremely creamy. It is wonderful to eat after dinner with a pear, but it is too creamy to use in a salad. We have found that American Gorgonzola has a firmer texture, is very tasty, and is much better for salads.

Longhi Salad

$1/2$ cup dried cannellini beans, or
   1 cup canned
1 head romaine lettuce
1 cup green beans
$1/2$ onion
1 tomato

DRESSING
2 tablespoons red wine vinegar
2 oil-packed anchovies, chopped
$1/2$ teaspoon Dijon mustard
$1/4$ cup Gorgonzola cheese
Freshly ground black pepper
6 tablespoons extra virgin olive oil

■ If you are using canned cannellini beans, drain them, rinse in cold water, and drain again. If you are using dried cannellini beans, soak them for 30 minutes and rinse in fresh water. Put them in a pot, add water to cover, and bring to a boil. Simmer the beans until soft, let cool, and refrigerate.

■ Wash and dry lettuce leaves, wrap with paper towels, and put in refrigerator. Steam green beans until cooked but still crisp; slice onion; cut tomato for salad.

■ Place the vinegar in a wooden salad bowl. Mash the anchovies into the vinegar with a fork. Whisk in the mustard, continuing until thoroughly incorporated. Add 2 tablespoons of the Gorgonzola cheese and mix well. Add fresh ground black pepper. Now add the olive oil, again mixing well.

■ Remove the lettuce from the refrigerator and cut the leaves into bite-sized pieces. Add the lettuce and the other vegetables and beans to the bowl and toss well with the dressing. Sprinkle salad with 2 tablespoons crumbled Gorgonzola cheese.

Serves 4

I HAVE ALWAYS BEEN a lover of Greek food, and one of my favorite things in a Greek restaurant is a Greek salad. The most important part of a Greek salad is the feta cheese. There are many varieties of feta cheese. There is Greek, Romanian, Bulgarian, American, and many other kinds. After experimenting I found that the best feta for salad was Romanian. Many people consider the Bulgarian feta the finest in the world. If you are going to eat the feta by itself, I would agree, but when it comes to a salad, I believe Romanian is better.

Greek Salad

1 head romaine lettuce

1 tomato

$^1/_2$ onion

1 cucumber

$^1/_4$ cup Greek olives

DRESSING

1 tablespoon lemon juice

1 tablespoon red wine vinegar

2 oil-packed anchovies

$^1/_4$ cup crumbled feta cheese

$^1/_2$ teaspoon oregano

Freshly ground black pepper

6 tablespoons extra virgin olive oil

■ Wash and dry lettuce; wrap leaves in paper towels and put in the refrigerator. Slice tomato, onion, and cucumber for salad.

■ Place the lemon juice and vinegar in a large wooden salad bowl, and whisk to mix well. With a fork, mash the anchovies into the lemon juice and vinegar. Add 2 tablespoons feta cheese, the oregano, and pepper, and mix well. Whisk in the olive oil.

■ Remove the lettuce from the refrigerator and cut the leaves into bite-sized pieces. Add the lettuce and the other vegetables to the bowl and toss well with the dressing. Sprinkle the salad with the remaining feta cheese and serve.

Serves 4

ONE OF MY FAVORITE SALADS is a Caesar salad. Americans love it too, so many restaurants serve a so-called Caesar salad. Unfortunately, most do not serve a true Caesar salad, which incorporates many things (including a one-minute egg) and, more importantly, must be tossed in a wooden bowl and immediately served.

My salad is not a Caesar salad, though it shares some of the ingredients. We do use Parmesan cheese, romaine lettuce, and anchovies. However, we do not use an egg. We call it a Longhi Longhi Longhi Salad. No one can say that it is not really a Longhi Longhi Longhi salad, because we are the experts on Longhi Longhi Longhi salads. We are the ones who created it, and therefore people can't say that it's not authentic because it doesn't have this or that in it.

Many people do not like anchovies, so we have the same salad with no anchovies, which in a flash of brilliance I named Longhi Longhi Longhi Salad.

Longhi Longhi Longhi Salad

1 head romaine lettuce

CROUTONS

1 small loaf Italian bread

1 stick ($^1/_2$ cup) butter

4 cloves garlic, chopped

1 tablespoon chopped parsley

DRESSING

1 tablespoon lemon juice

1 tablespoon red wine vinegar

$^1/_2$ teaspoon Dijon mustard

$^1/_2$ oil-packed anchovy, minced

4 tablespoons Parmigiano-Reggiano cheese

$^1/_2$ teaspoon oregano

Black pepper

6 tablespoons extra virgin olive oil

■ Wash and dry the lettuce, wrap leaves in paper towels and put in the refrigerator.

■ Preheat oven to 350°. Cut bread into $^1/_2$-inch-square cubes. Melt the butter. Add the garlic and sauté for 2 minutes; remove from heat. Add parsley. Toss bread cubes in garlic butter and bake in oven on a flat baking pan until golden brown.

■ Pour lemon juice and vinegar into a wooden salad bowl. Mix in the mustard, then add the anchovy and stir until it is incorporated into the vinegar. Add 2 tablespoons Parmesan cheese, oregano, and pepper and mix well. Now whisk in the olive oil. Cut the cold lettuce into pieces, add to the bowl and toss. Add 2 cups of the croutons and toss. Sprinkle the salad with the remaining Parmesan cheese and toss.

Serves 4

The New Cuisine of Longhi's

Starters

WHEN I OPENED LONGHI'S, my daughter Carol was seventeen and still in high school but wanted to work as a waitress at the restaurant. Carol's ebullient personality coupled with her sharp intellect made her a perfect candidate for a server at Longhi's. During her breaks from college, she worked at Longhi's as a waitress and manager, and later she became a full-time floor manager. Her interest in cooking intensified, and she began spending more and more time preparing special dishes for the restaurant or cooking for her own lavish parties. When Carol returned to Longhi's after working in the fashion industry for several years, she was drawn to the creative possibilities of cooking even more than before. She spent virtually all of her time in the kitchen at Longhi's and began to think seriously about a full-time career as a professional chef. In 1992, Carol approached me with the idea and told me she had done much research on the subject. She concluded that the place where she could get the best education was the Culinary Institute of America in Hyde Park, New York. This extensive, two-year program takes complete dedication and involves many hours of hard labor. During her second year at the Culinary Institute, Carol became pregnant with her second child. I remember calling her and asking, "Are there many other women in your school who have a child and are pregnant?" Carol replied, "I think I'm the first in the history of the school." Culinary school, unlike a liberal arts college, necessitates 10 to 12 hours of hard work almost every day of the week. I definitely didn't work that hard during my Ivy League tenure.

Carol graduated as one of the top students in her class, and since 1994 has been the chef at Longhi's—the first person I ever appointed to this position. Over the years, my kitchen has been run by a manager, not by an official chef. But Carol impressed me so much with her knowledge and talent after coming out of the CIA that I felt it was time to turn the reins over to her.

Carol's husband, Mark O'Leary, also attended the CIA. The two of them work extremely well together and have upgraded our food to even higher standards. Carol and Mark have now blessed me with three beautiful grandchildren. So I'm confident the culinary future of Longhi's is in good hands.

Prior to Carol's tenure as chef, Longhi's had few specially designated appetizers. One of Carol's first contributions was to introduce several tantalizing items. Potato-crusted crab cakes became an immediate sensation. In keeping with the Longhi tradition, Carol insists that we use only the finest crab for this dish. She also uses portobello mushrooms, fresh Pacific fish, lobster, and myriad other ingredients in her varied appetizer menu.

ABOUT AHI CARPACCIO

IN THE SUMMER OF 1995 I spent six weeks in Italy, traveling from Rome to Switzerland. When I left Geneva I drove back through Italy to San Remo, a medium-sized town on the Ligurian coast approximately 15 miles from France. I love Sam Remo for a number of reasons: it has a hotel that I particularly admire called the Royale; it is right next to the very expensive Côte d'Azur; it has great shopping at prices that are more reasonable than the large cities; and it has several great restaurants that showcase the fabulous Ligurian cuisine. Among them is a restaurant that is one of my top ten favorites. This restaurant, da Giannino, is run by Giuseppe and his wife, Anna, one of the great Ligurian chefs. It is reputed to be the only restaurant in Italy that makes the magnificent classical salad from the Genoa area called Cappon Magro. This is a fish and vegetable salad, possibly the most elaborate salad in the world. It contains so many different ingredients that it is not worth bothering with unless you are making it for at least twelve people. Basically the dish is made by cooking several different vegetables separately, doing the same with various kinds of Mediterranean seafood, saucing it all with an exotic mixture of parsley, garlic, anchovies, and pine nuts (combined with local Ligurian vinegar and olive oil), then putting it all together in the shape of a pyramid. Each Friday Anna labors many hours to make this rare masterpiece, and it is always completely sold out by Friday night.

Giuseppe and Anna also serve terrific trenette, which is a local variety of ribbon pasta that is known worldwide as the perfect accompaniment to pesto sauce. Needless to say, Anna makes

pesto as it should be made, using the classic recipe her mother taught her as a child. Anna also marries trenette with a black ink sauce made from the cuttlefish that are found in the harbor of San Remo. And I was especially pleased when Giuseppe informed me that Anna also prepares calves' brains cooked with burnt butter. I remembered that I had not enjoyed this delicacy since the early 1960s, when the great cook Maria made this dish every Wednesday in her restaurant in New York City, called Maria's.

Anna created a new dish called Pesce Carpaccio. This consisted of raw local fish served over bruschetta anointed with the wonderful extra virgin olive oil that comes from the hillsides surrounding San Remo. I was so enthralled that I ate it three days in a row. When I came back to Hawaii I described the dish to my chef, Carol, and asked her if she could reproduce it using Hawaiian fish and putting her own stamp of creativity upon it. Carol not only did this, but came up with a dish at least as good as the one in Italy, and one of our greatest appetizers.

Ahi Carpaccio

1 tomato, cut in small dice

$1/2$ cup plus 6 tablespoons extra
    virgin olive oil

$1/2$ cup loosely packed basil leaves

Salt and pepper

1 clove garlic, chopped

1 sprig rosemary, chopped

$1/2$ teaspoon fresh oregano

1 long loaf Italian bread, cut in $3/4$-inch
    slices (yields 8 to 12 slices)

$1/2$ pound sushi-grade ahi

3 cups baby salad greens

1 tablespoon lemon juice

2 lemons, halved

4 teaspoons capers

- In a bowl, toss the tomato with $1/4$ cup olive oil, the basil, and salt and pepper.

- Make the bruschetta. Combine $1/4$ cup extra virgin olive oil with garlic, rosemary, and oregano in a bowl. Brush both sides of each bread slice with the olive oil and herb mixture. Grill (or bake) the slices until golden brown, then turn slices over and grill the other side until golden brown.

- Slice the ahi—which should be very fresh and a deep ruby-red color, firm to the touch and almost translucent—about $1/8$ of an inch thick. It should be so thin you can read through it. Place 2 tablespoons of the tomato-basil mixture on each slice of grilled bread. Lay the slices of ahi over the tomatoes to cover each slice.

- Toss the salad greens with 2 tablespoons extra virgin olive oil and 1 tablespoon lemon juice, and salt and pepper. Place the greens on 4 plates and top with 2 to 3 pieces of bruschetta per plate. Squeeze juice from the lemon halves over the ahi, then drizzle with 1 tablespoon extra virgin olive oil per plate. Finally, sprinkle the top of the fish with capers, about 1 teaspoon per plate.

Serves 4

USE THE BEST CRABMEAT you can get for this dish—preferably fresh Maryland lump crabmeat. (This recipe is also wonderful with lobster.) Do not overmix or the crabmeat will merge into the bread crumbs. What you want are chunks of crab throughout the cakes. For variety Carol likes to substitute tarragon for the dill in both the crab cakes and the mustard sauce.

The tasty combination of very thin crusty potatoes covering fresh lump crabmeat is enhanced by the red pepper coulis and spicy mustard sauce, which do not overpower the delicate flavor of the crab.

Potato-Crusted Crab Cakes with Mustard Sauce and Red Pepper Coulis

4 russet potatoes

Vegetable oil (such as canola) for frying

1 shallot, finely diced

1 teaspoon salted butter

1 egg

1 teaspoon Worcestershire sauce

1 tablespoon lemon juice

2 teaspoons Colmans dry mustard

2 tablespoons mayonnaise

$1/4$ teaspoon cayenne pepper

$1/4$ teaspoon salt

$1/4$ teaspoon pepper

1 tablespoon fresh dill

1 pound Maryland lump crabmeat

$3/4$ cup bread crumbs

4 egg whites

Red Pepper Coulis (recipe follows)

Dijon Mustard Sauce (recipe follows)

■ Peel potatoes. Grate to a fine julienne with a mandoline or food processor; julienne should be 2 inches long and thickness of a matchstick. Cover potatoes with water to prevent browning.

■ Drain potatoes and dry thoroughly. Heat oil in a deep, heavy pan to a depth of 3 inches. Add potatoes and blanch 1 minute. Remove potatoes before they color and drain on paper towels. Let oil cool.

■ Sauté the shallot in butter until translucent; set aside. In a bowl, combine egg with Worcestershire sauce, lemon juice, dry mustard, mayonnaise, cayenne pepper, salt, and pepper; mix well. Add the shallot, dill, crabmeat, and bread crumbs and gently fold into wet ingredients until just combined. Do not overmix. The crabmeat should stay lumpy.

■ Shape crab mixture into eight $1^1/2$-ounce round but slightly flat patties. Set on a baking sheet and refrigerate 2 hours.

■ While crab cakes refrigerate, make the Red Pepper Coulis and the Dijon Mustard Sauce.

■ Beat 4 egg whites lightly. Dip crab cakes into egg whites, then roll in potatoes until coated.

■ Heat oil to 375°. Fry the crab cakes in oil until golden brown.

■ Cover each plate with half Dijon Mustard Sauce and half Red Pepper Coulis. Place two crab cakes in the center of each plate.

Serves 4

continued

Crab Cakes continued

Red Pepper Coulis

2 shallots, diced

2 tablespoons olive oil

1 clove garlic, chopped

1 jalapeño or serrano chile, chopped

3 red bell peppers, seeded and cut into
　　medium dice

$1/2$ cup white wine

1 cup heavy cream

2 tablespoons lemon juice

Salt and pepper

■ Sauté shallots in olive oil for 2 minutes. Add the garlic and sauté 1 minute. Add the chile and red peppers; sauté about 6 minutes until the peppers are soft. Add the white wine and reduce by two-thirds. Add the cream and let cook 3 minutes. Remove from heat and purée in a blender. Add lemon juice; season with salt and pepper.

Dijon Mustard Sauce

$1/2$ cup white wine

Juice of 1 lime

1 clove garlic, minced

1 shallot, chopped

1 bay leaf

2 cups heavy cream

2 tablespoons Dijon mustard

1 tablespoon Colmans dry mustard

Salt and pepper

1 tablespoon fresh dill

■ Add white wine, lime juice, garlic, shallot, and bay leaf to pan; simmer until reduced by three-fourths. Add cream and simmer until it thickens, about 5 minutes. Turn off heat, stir in mustards, and season with salt and pepper. Remove bay leaf. Purée sauce in blender and add fresh dill.

Grilled Mediterranean Shrimp with Minted White Beans

WHITE BEANS

1 cup dried white beans (small)

1 onion, coarsely chopped

1 carrot

1 stick celery

1 clove garlic

1 bay leaf

5 peppercorns

SHRIMP

$^1/_2$ cup olive oil

$^1/_4$ cup lemon juice

1 teaspoon chopped garlic

$^1/_4$ cup chopped flat-leaf parsley

$^1/_4$ cup mint, chopped

16 large shrimp (about 1$^1/_2$ pounds),
    shelled, cleaned, and deveined

DRESSING

$^1/_2$ cup extra virgin olive oil

4 tablespoons lemon juice

$^1/_2$ teaspoon chopped garlic

2 tablespoons chopped mint

2 tablespoons chopped flat-leaf parsley

Salt and pepper

1 tomato, diced

AIOLI

2 egg yolks

$^1/_2$ tablespoon wine vinegar

4 cloves garlic, mashed into a paste

Freshly ground black pepper (several
    twists of the mill)

1$^1/_2$ to 2 cups extra virgin olive oil

Lemon juice

Salt and pepper

■ Place beans in a pot and cover with 3 inches of water. Boil for 3 minutes. Turn off heat; let sit 1 hour. (Alternatively, soak the beans in water overnight.) Drain the beans and return to the pot, covering with 2 inches of fresh water. Add the remaining ingredients. Simmer until done, 40 to 90 minutes (no more than 60 minutes if beans are presoaked).

■ Drain the cooked beans, reserving $^1/_4$ cup of the cooking liquid. Add the reserved liquid to the beans and chill in the refrigerator.

■ To prepare the shrimp, combine the olive oil, lemon juice, garlic, parsley, and mint in a bowl. Add the shrimp and marinate for 30 minutes to 2 hours.

■ To make the dressing, combine all the ingredients except the tomato in a large bowl. Whisk together, then add the tomato and white beans and toss with the dressing.

■ To make the aioli, whisk together the egg yolks, vinegar, garlic, and pepper in a stainless steel bowl until foamy and lighter in color. Slowly whisk in the olive oil, until the mixture is the consistency of mayonnaise. Season with lemon juice, salt, and pepper to taste.

■ Grill shrimp on both sides until done. Put about $^1/_2$ cup of the bean mixture on each of 4 plates; for each serving, arrange 4 shrimp on top of the beans. Drizzle shrimp with aioli.

Serves 4

DON'T BE INTIMIDATED by this recipe. It's simple to make—there are just a few steps. You can roast the duck and make the crepes the day before. These duck rolls make a fabulous party appetizer. They take a little time to prepare but are well worth the effort.

Roasted Duck Rolls with Plum Sauce in Scallion Pancakes

1 duck (4 pounds)

$^1/_2$ teaspoon Chinese five-spice powder

SCALLION PANCAKES

3 eggs

2 tablespoons sesame oil

1 tablespoon peanut oil

$^2/_3$ cup milk

$^2/_3$ cup water

1 teaspoon salt

1 cup flour

2 scallions, green parts only, sliced into rings

$^1/_4$ cup vegetable oil

DUCK FILLING

2 tablespoons peanut oil

2 teaspoons minced ginger

3 cloves garlic, minced

4 scallions, white and green parts, sliced

$^1/_2$ teaspoon Chinese five-spice powder

1 tablespoon soy sauce

1 tablespoon rice wine vinegar

$^1/_2$ cup Thai plum sauce

$^1/_4$ cup hoisin sauce

1 cucumber, seeded and julienned into 2-inch-long matchsticks

■ Preheat oven to 375°. Score skin of duck and season with Chinese five-spice powder. Roast until internal temperature reaches 150° (about an hour). Remove duck from oven and let cool in the refrigerator.

■ To make the scallion pancakes, combine the eggs in a blender with the sesame oil, peanut oil, milk, and water, and blend. Add the salt and flour gradually, blending until the mixture is smooth. Transfer to a bowl and stir in the scallions. Refrigerate at least 1 hour.

- Heat a 6-inch crepe or nonstick pan and brush lightly with vegetable oil. The oil should be hot but not smoking. Pour about $1^1/_2$ ounces of batter into pan, enough to cover the bottom. Cook for 30 seconds to 1 minute, until the top side is dry; loosen the bottom of the pancake with a spatula, then flip and cook about 30 more seconds. Stack finished crepes between sheets of wax paper. Repeat until all the batter is used—this should make about 20 crepes. They can be wrapped and kept overnight in the refrigerator. Use the eye-appealing golden brown side for the outside of the pancake.

- To make the duck filling, pull the meat off the duck so that it is shredded. This is easiest when the duck has cooled before putting it in the refrigerator.

- Heat the peanut oil in a pan and add the ginger, garlic and scallions. Sauté for 2 to 3 minutes without browning the garlic. Add the duck and heat for a few minutes. Add five-spice powder, soy sauce, rice vinegar, Thai plum sauce, and hoisin sauce, and heat thoroughly.

- Place 1 heaping tablespoon of duck mixture and 5 cucumber matchsticks in the bottom third of each pancake. Leaving half an inch on either side for folding, roll the pancake (away from you) over once, then fold in both sides to seal the ends and continue to roll. Cut each roll in half diagonally and serve.

Serves 4

THESE MUSHROOMS ARE always a hit at parties and disappear unbelievably fast. Serving them on Gorgonzola-enriched polenta adds a creamy hardiness and contrasts nicely with the roasted garlic flavor absorbed by the mushrooms. Follow with an arugula salad (dressed with an extra virgin olive oil and balsamic vinaigrette) and crusty Italian bread. The grilled mushrooms are also fabulous served without the polenta.

Grilled Wild Mushrooms with Roasted Garlic and Grilled Polenta

$^1/_4$ cup toasted pine nuts

ROASTED GARLIC

1 head of garlic

$^1/_2$ cup extra virgin olive oil

POLENTA

6 cups water or chicken stock

2 cups polenta (coarse-grained cornmeal)

1 cup Gorgonzola cheese

$^1/_4$ cup Parmesan cheese

$^1/_4$ cup cream

1 tablespoon salt

Pepper to taste

$^1/_4$ cup extra virgin olive oil

GRILLED WILD MUSHROOMS

4 portobello mushrooms

$^1/_2$ pound shiitake mushrooms

$^1/_2$ cup extra virgin olive oil

$^1/_2$ teaspoon chopped rosemary plus

$^1/_2$ sprig, finely minced

2 cloves garlic, chopped

Juice of 1 lemon

2 tablespoons chopped flat-leaf parsley

Salt and pepper

■ Heat the oven to 350°. Place pine nuts on a baking sheet and toast in the oven about 10 minutes; do not scorch.

■ To roast the garlic, cut $^1/_4$ inch off the top of the garlic head. Place garlic in center of a 12 x 12-inch piece of foil on a baking sheet and pour the extra virgin olive oil on top of it. Wrap the garlic in the foil and roast in a 350° oven for about 1 hour, until the garlic is golden brown.

■ To make the polenta, bring the water or stock to a boil in a large pot. Turn heat down to a simmer and add the polenta in a thin steady stream while stirring constantly. Keep stirring for about 20 minutes, until the polenta pulls away from the sides of the pan. Stir in the cheeses, cream, and salt and pepper. Spread the mixture onto a baking tray and let set. Cut the polenta into squares, brushing each with extra virgin olive oil.

■ To prepare the grilled mushrooms, cut the stems off the portobello mushrooms and peel the skin off the top of each one. Pull the stems out of the shiitake mushrooms and save for other uses (such as vegetable stock).

■ Combine extra virgin olive oil, chopped rosemary, and garlic in a bowl. Brush the mushrooms, with this olive oil mixture. Grill the mushrooms, top side down, until lightly browned, then flip and cook until done (when they start releasing water and are soft). Remove mushrooms from grill and place in a pan.

■ Grill polenta squares until lightly browned.

■ Squeeze the garlic cloves out of the garlic head (along with the olive oil it baked in) directly into the pan with the grilled mushrooms. Add the lemon juice, $1/2$ sprig minced rosemary, chopped parsley, and salt and pepper. Mix gently.

■ Top the polenta squares with the grilled mushrooms; sprinkle with toasted pine nuts. Serve warm or at room temperature.

Serves 4

Grilled Vegetables with Goat Cheese Pesto

1 tablespoon pine nuts

GOAT CHEESE PESTO

$1/2$ cup extra virgin olive oil

2 cloves garlic, peeled

$1/2$ cup packed basil leaves

$1/4$ cup flat-leaf parsley

2 tablespoons goat cheese, such as
    Montrachet

Salt and pepper

VEGETABLES

1 eggplant

2 zucchini

1 red bell pepper

1 yellow bell pepper

1 onion

$1/2$ pound asparagus

1 clove garlic, chopped

1 teaspoon chopped basil

1 teaspoon chopped oregano

$1/2$ cup olive oil

1 loaf crusty Italian bread

■ Toast the pine nuts on a baking sheet in a 350° oven until brown, 5 to 10 minutes. They burn quickly so you will need to check them. Remove them from oven and let cool.

■ To make the pesto, throw all ingredients except the cheese, salt, and pepper into a blender and purée until creamy. Add the cheese and blend again until it is incorporated into the mixture. Season with salt and pepper. Do not overblend.

■ To prepare the grilled vegetables, cut the eggplant crosswise and on the bias into $1/3$-inch-thick slices. Slice the zucchini lengthwise into $1/3$-inch-thick strips. Slice the peppers into rounds. Cut the onion into $1/3$-inch-thick slices. Cut off the ends of the asparagus. Mix the garlic, basil, oregano, and olive oil in a bowl. Brush the vegetables with the oil mixture, coating all sides. Grill the vegetables on a medium-hot grill until cooked. Season with salt and pepper and drizzle with Goat Cheese Pesto. Serve with the bread.

Serves 4

ARUGULA AND CARAMELIZED macadamia nuts make this light salad sweet and spicy at the same time.

Kula Green Salad

DRESSING

2 tablespoons wine vinegar

2 tablespoons sherry vinegar

1 tablespoon shoyu or soy sauce

1 tablespoon sesame oil

1 teaspoon honey

2 teaspoons dry mustard

1 scallion, chopped

8 leaves fresh mint

1 small clove garlic, chopped

1 cup olive oil

CARAMELIZED MACADAMIA NUTS

$1/2$ cup sugar

$1/2$ cup water

$1/4$ cup chopped roasted macadamia nuts

SALAD GREENS

4 cups baby greens

$1/2$ cup young arugula

■ To make the dressing, blend all listed ingredients together, adding the olive oil last.

■ To make the caramelized macadamia nuts, preheat the oven to 350°. Combine sugar and water in a saucepan; let boil 1 minute and add the nuts. Simmer nuts until they are caramelized and light brown in color. Pour onto a baking sheet and bake until nuts are brown and crunchy, about 10 minutes.

■ Toss salad greens with the dressing and sprinkle with the caramelized nuts.

Serves 4

Entrées

CAROL HAS ADDED MANY EXCITING new creations to the old standbys of Longhi's—Grilled Vegetable Pasta (opposite page), Mint Pesto (page 114), various risottos, and several new seafood dishes. The following are some of her most popular and easy-to-make recipes.

CAROL LIKES TO USE Asiago cheese to bring a slightly more assertive flavor to this dish, although feta or Parmesan can be used with equally satisfying results. The sauce is also good the next day, served on crusty Italian bread.

Grilled Vegetable Pasta

1 medium eggplant, cut crosswise
   into $1/3$-inch-thick slices
2 medium zucchini, cut crosswise
   into $1/3$-inch-thick slices
1 red bell pepper, seeded and cut
   into 1-inch-wide strips
1 yellow bell pepper, seeded and cut
   into 1-inch-wide strips
1 red onion, peeled and cut into
   $1/4$-inch-thick rings
$3/4$ cup olive oil
1 teaspoon salt
Dash of olive oil
1 pound spaghetti
4 cloves garlic, chopped
$1/4$ cup chopped flat-leaf parsley
1 teaspoon crushed red pepper flakes
8 ounces shiitake, porcini, morel, or
   button mushrooms, sliced
3 cups Pomodoro Sauce (page 23)
$1/4$ cup chopped basil
$1/2$ cup grated Asiago, or Parmesan, or
   crumbled feta cheese
Red peppercorns

■ Brush all vegetables with $1/2$ cup of the olive oil and grill or broil them until they are golden brown, about 5 minutes. (If using a broiler, make sure the vegetables are close to the flame.) Remove grilled vegetables from heat and chop into $1/2$-inch bite-sized strips.

■ Fill a large stainless steel pot with water and bring to a boil. Add salt and a dash of olive oil, then drop in the spaghetti.

■ Heat the remaining $1/4$ cup olive oil in a pan; add the chopped garlic, half of the parsley, and the crushed red pepper flakes. Add the mushrooms and sauté lightly. Add Pomodoro Sauce, grilled vegetables, and the remainder of the herbs. Add the cooked spaghetti to the pan and toss with the cheese. Serve with a few twists of cracked red pepper.

Serves 4

Mint pesto is an interesting switch from the standard version made with basil. This refreshing dish can be the centerpiece of a wonderful summer meal when mint is abundant. Serve with a vine-ripened tomato salad sprinkled with olive oil, vinegar, salt, and freshly ground pepper to make a perfect hot-weather feast.

Mint Pesto with Linguine

1 tablespoon pine nuts

$1/3$ cup plus 1 tablespoon olive oil

$1/2$ cup mint, packed

$1/2$ cup flat-leaf parsley, packed

1 teaspoon garlic

$1/4$ to $1/2$ teaspoon plus 1 teaspoon salt

Freshly ground black pepper

1 pound linguine

$1/2$ cup grated Parmigiano-Reggiano or
   crumbled feta cheese

■ Toast pine nuts on a baking sheet in a 350° oven until golden brown, about 10 minutes. Blend olive oil, mint, parsley, garlic, pine nuts, $1/4$ teaspoon salt, and $1/4$ teaspoon pepper in a blender or food processor. Add salt to taste if needed.

■ Fill a large stainless steel pot with water and bring to a boil. Add 1 teaspoon salt and 1 tablespoon olive oil, then drop the linguine into the boiling water until cooked to taste. When linguine is ready, take 2 tablespoons of the hot water it cooked in and mix it into the pesto. Toss the linguine with the pesto and Parmesan or feta cheese. Season to taste with additional black pepper.

Serves 4

THESE ONIONS MUST BE COOKED slowly to develop their full sweetness. The mozzarella makes a mellow background for the savory rosemary and sweet onion flavors.

Caramelized Five-Onion Ravioli

RAVIOLI PASTA DOUGH

2 cups all-purpose flour

3 eggs

1 tablespoon milk

ONION AND MUSHROOM MIXTURE

2 tablespoons plus $1/4$ cup extra
  virgin olive oil

$1/2$ medium-sized red onion, sliced

$1/4$ white onion, sliced

3 leeks, white part only, sliced

4 shallots, sliced

3 scallions, white parts only, sliced

1 teaspoon chopped garlic

$1/2$ teaspoon rosemary, finely chopped

$1/2$ pound shiitake mushrooms, stems
  removed, tops sliced

1 teaspoon lemon juice

$1/4$ cup white wine

Salt and pepper

$1 1/2$ cups ricotta cheese

$1/2$ cup crumbled feta cheese

$1/2$ cup shredded mozzarella cheese

$1/4$ cup grated Parmigiano-Reggiano
  cheese

1 egg

1 tablespoon chopped flat-leaf parsley

1 egg, beaten lightly

1 teaspoon salt

1 tablespoon olive oil

PARSLEY SAUCE

$1/4$ cup pine nuts

$1/2$ cup extra virgin olive oil

1 cup loosely packed flat-leaf parsley
  leaves

$1/2$ cup Parmigiano-Reggiano cheese

Freshly ground black pepper

■ To make the pasta, make a pile with the flour. Make a well in the center and add the eggs, beating them with a fork. Add the milk. Work the flour into the eggs and form a ball. Knead dough for 8 minutes. Let it rest 30 minutes in the refrigerator, then remove and let sit at room temperature for 10 minutes.

■ To make the onion-mushroom mixture, sauté onions in 2 tablespoons of the olive oil over low heat until caramelized, about 20 to 30 minutes. In another pan, sauté garlic and rosemary in the remaining $1/4$ cup olive oil; add sliced mushrooms and sauté 2 minutes. Add the lemon juice and white wine, and saute until liquids are absorbed, 2 to 3 minutes. Turn off the heat and season with salt and pepper.

■ Chop cooked mushrooms into small pieces, then combine with the onions. In another bowl, mix the cheeses together then add 1 egg. Add the onion-mushroom mixture to the cheeses and mix well. Add chopped parsley and salt and pepper to taste.

■ Cut pasta dough into 8 pieces. Working quickly, put the dough through a pasta machine, progressively rolling it thinner until you have run the dough through the lowest setting and you can see through it. Keep the dough about 3 inches wide. Lay the dough on a floured board. Roll out the next piece and place it next to the first. Brush pasta with beaten egg.

■ Place 1 tablespoon of cheese-onion mixture on one of the rolled-out pieces of pasta every couple of inches. Lay the second piece over it and press down to release the air. Cut all edges with a ravioli cutter (or trim sides with a knife) and press down with the tines of a fork to create a scalloped edge. Repeat until all the dough and onion-mushroom mixture is used. Makes about 24 ravioli.

■ Boil ravioli in water with 1 tablespoon olive oil and 1 teaspoon salt until done, about 5 minutes.

■ To make the Parsley Sauce, toast pine nuts in a 350° oven for 10 minutes. Heat olive oil until shimmering but not smoking. Fry parsley until crisp, about 10 seconds. Sauce ravioli with 2 to 3 tablespoons parsley oil, a sprinkle of Parmesan cheese, and freshly ground pepper. Top with toasted pine nuts.

Serves 4

RISOTTO IS A CLASSIC DISH served throughout northern Italy. It is typically made with Arborio, a highly glutenous rice grown in the Po Valley of northern Italy. Roma and Canaroli are other types of Italian rice that can be used. If you want this dish to be authentic, you must use Italian rice. This rice absorbs the flavors of the ingredients with which it is cooked, while each grain remains firm. The combination of full flavor, al dente rice, and a luxurious creamy consistency is what gives risotto its unique, soul-satisfying character. Risotto cannot be cooked in the microwave, but must be stirred over the stove with full attention, while the cook adds liquid, half a cup at a time for about 20 minutes, until the rice has reached perfection. Risotto can stand on its own or accompany a variety of foods, such as grilled swordfish, roasted chicken, or veal chops.

Artichoke and Wild Mushroom Risotto

5 large globe artichokes

Lemon juice

1 pound wild mushrooms, such as shiitake, hedgehog, or morel

1 tablespoon olive oil

7 tablespoons sweet butter

1/2 onion, cut into small dice

1 clove garlic, minced

1/4 cup chopped flat-leaf parsley

6 cups vegetable stock

2 cups Arborio rice

1/2 cup dry white wine

1/2 cup Parmigiano-Reggiano cheese

Salt and pepper

■ To prepare each artichoke, cut off the stem and remove all the outer leaves. In the center of the artichoke will be some purple leaves with sharp tips; cut off all these leaves and then scrape out the fuzzy choke beneath them so you have only the uncooked artichoke heart. Slice the artichoke heart thin and place in a bowl; cover with water. Add a squeeze of lemon juice to the water; this will prevent the artichokes from oxidizing and turning brown. Prepare the remaining artichokes the same way.

■ To prepare the mushrooms, remove stems and cut up to use in the risotto base. (Do not use shiitake stems, however, which are woody and not good to eat.) Put chopped stems in a bowl. Quarter the mushroom tops and put in another bowl.

■ To a sauté pan over medium heat, add the olive oil and 3 tablespoons of the butter. When the butter has melted, add the onion and sauté for 3 minutes. Add the garlic and 2 tablespoons of the chopped parsley and sauté 2 minutes. Add the sliced artichokes and sauté 1 minute. Add $1/2$ cup of the stock and cover the pan for 15 minutes, until the artichokes are soft. When they are almost cooked, add the mushroom stems and sauté 1 minute. Cover until artichokes are done—that is, when the heart can be pierced by a fork—adding liquid or butter as needed.

■ In a separate pan, sauté the mushroom tops in 3 tablespoons of the butter until done. Add a squeeze of lemon at the end. Remove from heat and set aside.

■ To the sauté pan containing the artichokes, add 2 cups of arborio rice. Stir the rice over medium heat until it is coated with oil; mix 1 to 2 minutes. Add white wine and stir until liquid is absorbed. Then add the vegetable stock 1 cup at a time, stirring constantly until the liquid is absorbed. Only add more broth when all previous liquid has been absorbed by the rice. Keep adding broth and stirring until the rice is cooked. The rice should have a firm but chewy texture, soft on the outside but with a firm center. The consistency of the rice in the pan should be creamy. This process takes 18 to 25 minutes.

■ When the rice is finished, turn the heat low and add the sautéed mushroom tops; mix into rice. Turn off the heat and add Parmesan cheese, the remaining 1 tablespoon butter and 2 tablespoons parsley. Mix for 30 seconds. Season with salt and pepper.

Serves 4

SHUTOME IS HAWAIIAN Pacific swordfish. You can easily substitute Atlantic swordfish for it. When choosing the fish, look for a "blood line," a fresh, clean smell, and translucent flesh that is firm to the touch.

Shutome with Cilantro Butter

MARINADE

2 cloves garlic

1 teaspoon chopped ginger

2 whole scallions

$1/2$ teaspoon red pepper flakes

1 tablespoon soy sauce

Juice of 2 limes

$1/2$ cup olive oil

CILANTRO BUTTER

1 stick ($1/2$ cup) salted butter, at room
   temperature

$1/4$ cup cilantro leaves

1 scallion, green parts only

1 clove garlic

Juice of 1 lime

1 teaspoon soy sauce

$1/2$ teaspoon salt

Black pepper

2 pounds shutome, cut into
   $1/4$-inch-thick fillets

1 large onion, sliced into $1/4$-inch
   thick rings

1 large red bell pepper, cut into $1/4$-inch
   thick slices

1 large yellow bell pepper, cut into
   $1/4$-inch thick slices

- To make the marinade, combine garlic, ginger, scallions, and red pepper in a food processor. Pulse, then add soy sauce, lime juice, and olive oil, and pulse until combined. Coat the fish with the marinade and marinate in the refrigerator for 1 to 4 hours.

- To make the cilantro butter, combine all listed ingredients until incorporated. Roll butter in plastic wrap to form a log. Wrap well and immerse in ice water to quickly harden.

- Grill shutome, onion, and bell peppers on hot grill until almost done. Cut butter log into four $1/4$-inch disks, placing a disk on top of each fish fillet 1 minute before it is done grilling. (Cook fish for about 10 minutes per inch of thickness.)

Serves 4

A GREAT LAMB CHOP doesn't need much. This is a spin on the classic mint sauce. The addition of the fruit adds a delicate tartness that complements the earthy flavor of the lamb.

Many people think that lamb from Australia and New Zealand is the best. I beg to differ, as we have found that the best lamb comes from America; it is much juicier than the Down Under variety and does not have a gamy taste. Many restaurants brag about using Australian or New Zealand lamb, but in reality it is a much less expensive product than American lamb. The most expensive lamb that you can buy is from the United States. One of our simplest but most sought-after dishes is beautiful loin lamb chops broiled and served with a mint sauce.

Grilled Lamb Chops with Raspberry-Mint Sauce

1 cup raspberry wine vinegar

1 cup rice wine vinegar

2 cups sugar

1^1/$_2$ cups packed, coarsely chopped mint leaves, stems reserved

^{1}/$_4$ cup Chambord (raspberry) liqueur

8 1^1/$_2$-inch-thick loin lamb chops

1 pint raspberries

■ In a small, nonreactive saucepan, whisk together the vinegars and sugar. Simmer over medium heat for 2 minutes. Add the chopped mint leaves and stems, then add the Chambord and simmer until the mixture thickens. Remove from the heat and let cool. Stain the liquid to remove the mint. Set aside until ready to sauce the chops, or store in an airtight container in the refrigerator for up to 2 weeks.

■ Prepare grill or broiler. Cook the lamb chops to desired doneness. Serve with the sauce and a sprinkle of fresh raspberries.

Serves 4

I LOVE THE SWEET-AND-SOUR flavor of fruit with grilled duck. I like to serve this dish with rosemary- and garlic- flavored mashed potatoes and baked acorn squash with maple syrup.

Crispy Duck with Raspberry-Ginger-Orange Sauce

2 large boneless duck breasts, skin on

1 teaspoon vegetable oil

1 shallot, minced

1 teaspoon finely minced fresh ginger

1 teaspoon brown sugar

$1/2$ cup good-quality Merlot wine

$1/4$ cup freshly squeezed orange juice

$1/4$ cup chicken stock

1 ounce Chambourg (raspberry) liqueur

$1/4$ cup heavy cream

1 tablespoon cold butter, cut into chunks

$1/2$ cup fresh raspberries

Salt and pepper

■ Preheat oven to 350°. Puncture the duck skin with a fork. Heat the oil in a sauté pan until hot but not smoking. Add duck, skin side down, and render fat. This should take about 10 minutes. The skin should be crispy and golden brown when done. Place the duck on a roasting pan and roast to medium-rare, about 15 minutes.

■ While the duck is roasting, clean the sauté pan, then add the shallot and ginger, and sweat over low heat for about 1 minute. Add the sugar and then the wine, and increase the heat to medium-high. Reduce by two-thirds. Add the orange juice, reduce by half, and then add the chicken stock and reduce by half. Add the heavy cream and Chambourg, lower heat to medium, and simmer sauce until it is saucy and thick enough to coat the back of a spoon. Whisk in the butter. Finally, add the berries and season with salt and pepper.

■ Slice the breasts on the bias and fan out half a breast on each plate.

Serves 4

Grilled Chicken Breasts with Mediterranean Salsa on Focaccia with Aioli

MEDITERRANEAN SALSA

1 red onion, peeled and quartered

2 tomatoes

4 cloves garlic

$1/4$ cup extra virgin olive oil

2 jalapeño chiles

1 red bell pepper

1 yellow bell pepper

1 tablespoon chopped mint

1 tablespoon chopped flat-leaf parsley

Salt and pepper

MARINADE

$1/4$ cup olive oil

Juice of 1 lemon

1 teaspoon chopped rosemary

2 cloves garlic, chopped

$1/2$ teaspoon crushed red pepper flakes

1 teaspoon chopped flat-leaf parsley

$1/2$ teaspoon salt

4 boneless, skinless chicken breasts

AIOLI

2 egg yolks

$1/2$ tablespoon wine vinegar

4 cloves garlic, mashed into a paste

Several twists of freshly ground black pepper

$1^1/2$ to 2 cups extra virgin olive oil

Lemon juice

Salt and pepper

1 loaf focaccia bread

■ To make the salsa, heat oven to 350°. Place onion, tomatoes, and garlic in a baking pan and drizzle with extra virgin olive oil. Bake about 1 hour, until the onion is caramelized.

■ Next, grill or broil the chiles and peppers until skins are charred, and place them under a bowl for 5 minutes. Remove the bowl, peel and seed the chiles and bell peppers, and chop them into a small dice. Chop the baked onion, garlic, and tomatoes into dice of the same size. Put all of the vegetables in a bowl with the olive oil from the baking pan and mix. Add the mint, parsley, and salt and pepper to taste.

■ To make the marinade, combine all ingredients in a bowl. Pour over the chicken breasts and marinate in the refrigerator for 2 to 4 hours.

■ To make the aioli, combine egg yolks, vinegar, garlic, and pepper in a stainless steel bowl. Whisk together until mixture is foamy and has lightened in color. Add olive oil slowly in a steady stream, whisking continuously until the mixture is the consistency of mayonnaise. Season with lemon juice, salt, and pepper to taste.

■ Pound the chicken breasts until they are an even $1/3$ inch thick. Grill or broil until cooked.

■ Cut focaccia bread for sandwiches. Place chicken on bread and top with Mediterranean salsa; drizzle with aioli.

Serves 4

Desserts

CAROL WAS ACTUALLY INTERESTED in baking before she attended the Culinary Institute. Even though we have a great pastry chef, Carol wanted to add some of her favorite recipes to our menu. She uses most of the following desserts in our catering business, which has blossomed tremendously since its inception.

MASCARPONE CHEESE IS THE secret to the luxurious creamy texture of this cheesecake. Use fresh cream cheese that has not been stabilized with gelatin.

This ricotta cheesecake has a unique moussey texture. The addition of chocolate, mascarpone cheese, and orange zest makes it luxuriously haunting. Do not refrigerate the cake until it has cooled, or it will lose its delicate texture.

Chocolate-Orange Ricotta Cheesecake

CRUST

$3/4$ cup hazelnuts

8 biscotti cookies

1 stick ($1/2$ cup) sweet butter, cut into chunks

$1/3$ cup sugar

CAKE BATTER

3 ounces bittersweet chocolate

$1 1/2$ pounds ricotta cheese

$1/2$ pound mascarpone cheese

$3/4$ cup sugar

Juice and zest of 1 orange

$1/4$ cup Cointreau

1 teaspoon vanilla

$1/4$ cup all-purpose flour

3 large eggs, at room temperature

■ To make the crust, chop nuts in a food processor. Add cookies and chop. Add butter and sugar and process until incorporated. Press into a buttered 10-inch cake pan so that the crust is $1/16$ inch thick and comes $3/4$ of the way up the sides of the pan.

■ Preheat oven to 350°.

■ To make the cake batter, melt the chocolate in the top of a double boiler and remove from heat. Combine ricotta and mascarpone cheeses in a bowl; beat with a paddle attachment on low speed until combined. Add the sugar and beat until dissolved, about 4 minutes. Add the orange juice and zest, Cointreau, vanilla, and flour. Scrape down the bowl.

■ Add the eggs one at a time, beating until incorporated, 1 minute for each egg. Scrape the bowl and add the melted chocolate; beat until thoroughly blended. Pour the batter into the prepared cake pan.

■ Set the pan in a roasting pan and pour hot water into the roasting pan so that it reaches halfway up the sides. Bake in the center of the oven for 50 to 60 minutes, until the cake sets. The top will puff, and slight cracks and blisters will appear on top of the cake. It should quiver slightly when shaken.

■ Cool the cake to room temperature before refrigerating to preserve its creamy texture.

Makes one 10-inch cheesecake

Amaretto-Lemon Cheesecake

CRUST

10 graham crackers

$^1/_2$ cup slivered blanched almonds

$^1/_3$ cup sugar

$^1/_2$ cup butter

CHEESECAKE MIXTURE

1 pound ricotta cheese

$^1/_2$ pound cream cheese

$^1/_2$ pound mascarpone

$^3/_4$ cup sugar

Juice and zest of 1 lemon

1 teaspoon vanilla

1 tablespoon flour

$^1/_4$ cup Amaretto

3 large eggs

CARAMELIZED ALMOND TOPPING

1 cup water

1 cup sugar

1 cup slivered blanched almonds

■ To make the crust, combine graham crackers and almonds and chop in a food processor. Add the sugar and butter and process until combined. Press mixture into a buttered 10-inch cake pan so that the crust is $^1/_{16}$ inch thick and comes $^3/_4$ of the way up the sides of the pan.

■ Preheat oven to 350°.

■ To make the cheesecake, combine the cheeses in a bowl and beat with a paddle attachment on low setting until completely smooth, about 3 minutes. Add the sugar and beat until dissolved. Scrape the bowl and add lemon juice and zest, vanilla, flour, and Amaretto. Blend until incorporated. Add eggs one at a time, blending on low speed about 1 minute between each addition.

■ Pour the batter into the prepared cake pan. Place cake pan in a roasting pan in the center of the oven. Fill roasting pan halfway with water. Bake 50 to 60 minutes, until cake is puffed around the edges and moves slightly when shaken.

■ For the topping, combine water and sugar in a pan and stir 1 minute over medium heat. Add almonds and cook until liquid turns a light golden brown. Remove from heat and strain liquid out of the pan. Pour onto an ungreased baking sheet and spread thin. Set aside to cool. When set, break into 3-inch squares and place on the top of the cake.

Makes one 10-inch cheesecake

WHEN CAROL WAS AT THE CULINARY Institute of America in Hyde Park, New York, she was lucky to live in an area that produces many outstanding apple varieties harvested from early autumn right through Christmas. She had her pick of Stayman Winesaps, Northern Spies, and Ida Reds at roadside farm stands all through the fall. These apples, brilliantly crisp and amazingly fresh, make glorious pies. You can use any crisp, fresh apples, such as Granny Smith, Gravenstein, or Jonathan varieties, and pair this pie with cinnamon-clove ice cream. This combination reminds her of those beautifully vigorous and crisp East Coast autumn days.

Hudson River Valley Apple Pie with Cinnamon-Clove Ice Cream

PIE CRUST

1 1/2 cups all-purpose or pastry flour

1 teaspoon salt

1 tablespoon sugar

1 stick (1/2 cup) cold unsalted butter, cut into 24 pieces

1/4 cup ice water

APPLE PIE FILLING

6 to 7 medium to large apples

Juice and zest of 1 lemon

1/2 cup sugar

1/2 teaspoon ground allspice

1 teaspoon ground cinnamon

3 tablespoons flour

2 tablespoons sweet butter, cut into small chunks

1 egg

■ To make the crust, combine the flour, salt, and sugar. Mix on low speed with a paddle attachment, pulse in a food processor, or mix with your hands until combined. Add cold butter and mix, pulse, cut with two knives, or mix with fingers until the mixture resembles coarse meal. Add ice water and blend only until incorporated and the pastry holds together. Do not overmix. (This is the secret of flaky pastry.) Cut the pastry into two pieces, one larger and one smaller; smash them flat and wrap them in wax paper. Let the pastry rest in the refrigerator 30 minutes to 1 hour.

■ Meanwhile, to make the pie filling, preheat oven to 375°. Peel and core the apples, cut them into eighths, and put them in a bowl. Sprinkle lemon juice and zest over apples. Add sugar, spices, and flour, and mix.

■ Roll out the larger half of pastry dough into a round, $1/8$-inch-thick bottom crust. Fold it in half and transfer to a 8-inch pie tin; press into tin and form edges. Pierce the bottom a few times with a fork. Roll out the smaller piece of pie dough and cut into 10 strips that will form a lattice top.

■ Fill the crust with the apple filling; dot with butter. Place 5 strips of dough over the pie. Weave the 5 remaining strips through the strips on the pie. Beat the egg in a bowl and brush over the pastry. Bake the pie for 45 minutes to 1 hour. Serve with Cinnamon and Cloves Ice Cream.

Makes one 8-inch pie

Cinnamon-Clove Ice Cream

$2/3$ **cup sugar**

3 cups heavy cream

1 cup milk

1 vanilla bean

4 egg yolks

2 teaspoons ground cinnamon

$1/2$ **teaspoon ground cloves**

■ Place $1/3$ cup of the sugar in the top of a double boiler. Stir in the cream and the milk and bring to a simmer. Add the vanilla bean.

■ In a medium stainless steel mixing bowl, beat together the egg yolks and the remaining $1/3$ cup sugar. Slowly add $1/4$ cup of the hot milk mixture, while beating continuously. Stir in the rest of the liquid, a little at a time, until all of it is incorporated. Add the cinnamon and cloves.

■ Prepare an ice bath that can hold the stainless mixing bowl. Place the stainless bowl over the bottom of the double boiler, making sure the water does not touch the bottom of the bowl. Stir and cook until the mixture is thick enough to coat the back of a spoon. Transfer to the ice bath and let rest until cool. Remove vanilla bean, then freeze the mixture in an ice cream maker according to manufacturer's instructions.

Makes 2 quarts

CAROL MADE THESE COOKIES on the fly for a party she catered. She was in need of a dessert and they were simple to make. They flew off the tray, and every time she serves them, somebody is stuck munching away on these addicting cookies. They always disappear quickly with requests for more.

Chocolate-Dipped Macaroons

5 egg whites

2 cups powdered sugar, sifted

2 cups finely ground almonds

4 cups shredded sweetened coconut

Zest of $1/2$ lemon

$1^1/_2$ tablespoons dark rum

4 ounces semisweet chocolate

■ Line a baking sheet with waxed paper. Preheat oven to 300°.

■ Beat egg whites until stiff peaks form. Fold the almonds and add the coconut, the remaining 1 cup of powdered sugar, the lemon zest and rum. Spoon teaspoon-sized drops onto the baking sheet. Bake for 20 minutes, or until golden brown on the outside and soft on the inside. Cool on the baking sheet.

■ Place the chocolate in the top of a double boiler and set over gently simmering water. Stir occasionally as chocolate melts. When melted, lower heat to warm. Alternatively, microwave on high for 30 seconds, then check to see if melted. If not melted, stir and microwave for another 30 seconds.

■ Dip macaroons into the melted chocolate, coating one-third to one-half of each cookie. Place dipped cookies on waxed paper to set. Serve when chocolate is firm.

Makes 3 dozen cookies

Chocolate-Dipped Strawberries

1 pound semisweet dipping chocolate
20 long-stemmed strawberries, rinsed
and dried well

≈

▪ Chop the chocolate into 1-inch pieces. Place the chocolate in the top of a double boiler and set over gently simmering water. Stir occasionally as chocolate melts. As soon as the chocolate is melted, lower the heat to warm. Alternatively, microwave on high for 30 seconds, then check to see whether it has melted. If not melted, stir and microwave for another 30 seconds.

▪ Dip the strawberries in the chocolate, leaving one-quarter uncoated, then set the dipped strawberries on waxed paper. Place in the refrigerator to set. Serve when chocolate is firm.

Makes 20 dipped strawberries

Old Favorites from Longhi's Bakery

Baked Goods and Sweets

ONE OF THE MOST APPEALING things about eating at Longhi's has always been the fantastic desserts, breads, and pastries produced by our baking department. Credit for the genesis of the baking department belongs to Randi Humm. Randi and I lived together for more than 6 years. She was with me when I came to Maui and discovered 888 Front Street, the future site of Longhi's. Randi was a wonderful cook and a fabulous baker. The first decision we made regarding the bakery was that we would make all our own desserts and bake our own bread. From Longhi's opening day, our bakery has made us completely self-sufficient in this area.

When Randi decided to leave the island, our department floundered for a few days. Then another Randy—Randy Ortega—came to work at Longhi's. Randy had 10 years of experience at large bakeries, hotels, and restaurants, and he specialized in cake and bread making.

Randy tells the story of how he bought a one-way ticket to Maui knowing that this would be the place where he would spend his future. On his first day here he was sitting on the beach, and he asked one of the surfers to name the best restaurant on Maui. The surfer told him Longhi's. Randy walked in the next day, talked to me for fifteen minutes, and I immediately hired him. This turned out to be one of the best decisions I've ever made.

Randy has developed more than two thousand different desserts, several kinds of bread, and some of the most beautiful ice cream and sorbet one can eat. Unlike many pastry chefs, he has a completely open mind. I read many cookbooks and eat at many restaurants, so I often come up with new ideas. I then go to Randy and tell him about a particular dish I've gotten excited about. In every instance Randy has researched the recipe or, in many cases, created one from his own imagination. I must say that he always succeeds. Randy has worked for me for more than fifteen years, and he has not only been a terrific pastry chef, but also manages his staff of six in an exemplary manner.

Spinach Spanakopita Quiche

CRUST

3 cups all-purpose flour

$2/3$ cup butter

$2/3$ cup shortening

1 teaspoon salt

$1/2$ cup water

Juice of $1/2$ lemon

SPINACH FILLING

$1^1/2$ cups chopped onion

$1/4$ cup olive oil

3 cups packed chopped fresh spinach

$1^1/2$ teaspoons dill

2 cups heavy cream

6 eggs

Pepper

Salt

1 cup shredded mozzarella

$2/3$ cup crumbled feta cheese

■ To make the crust, mix flour, butter, and shortening until mealy. Add salt, water, and lemon juice; mix by hand. Refrigerate for 1 hour. Divide dough in half. Roll out one piece of dough into a large circle big enough to cover the bottom and sides of a 9-inch-diameter, $2^1/2$-inch-deep pie pan. Line the pan with the dough and crimp edges. (Note: This recipe makes enough for two pie crusts, although you will only need one. The extra crust may be shaped into a disc, covered in plastic wrap, and refrigerated for several days.)

■ To make the spinach filling, sauté the onion in the olive oil until translucent. Add the spinach and sauté until wilted. Add the fresh dill and remove pan from heat. In a bowl, mix the heavy cream with the eggs. Season with salt and pepper.

■ Preheat the oven to 350°. Add the cheeses to the bottom of the pie and spread evenly, topping with the sautéed spinach mixture. Pour the egg mixture into the pie pan. Bake the quiche for 1 hour and 20 minutes, or until set in the middle. Cool on a wire rack, then unmold and serve.

Serves 4 to 6

JALAPEÑO CHEESE BREAD was Randy Ortega's first contribution to the restaurant, and we still serve it. People often say, "I came all the way from _____ just for the Jalapeño Cheese Bread."

Jalapeño Cheese Bread

1 (3.5-ounce) can jalapeño chiles
2 (4-ounce) cans green chiles

BREAD

1 teaspoon salt
1 teaspoon sugar
1 package dry active yeast
2 cups bread flour
1 cup water

1¹/₂ cups shredded mozzarella cheese

■ Drain the jalapeños and green chiles and chop. Combine in a bowl.

■ To prepare the bread, place all dry ingredients in a large bowl and mix with water. If you have a mixer, use the dough attachment and mix until the dough is smooth. If you use your hands, mix until the dough is smooth and no longer sticks to your hands. Let the dough relax for 15 minutes, then form into a long 12- to 15-inch loaf. Let the loaf rise until it has doubled in size. With a sharp knife, cut down the middle of the loaf to make a crevice about ¹/₂ inch deep. Fill the crevice with the green chile and jalapeño mixture. Top the loaf with shredded mozzarella. Bake in a 350° oven for 18 minutes, or until brown. Remove and let cool for 5 minutes. Cut and serve.

Makes one 12-inch loaf

Randalino

PIZZA DOUGH

2 cups bread flour

1 teaspoon sugar

1 teaspoon salt

1 package dry active yeast

1 cup water

PIZZA SAUCE

1 (10-ounce) can diced tomatoes

4 cloves garlic, finely diced

$1/4$ cup olive oil

2 tablespoons chopped oil-packed
    anchovies

1 tablespoon crushed red pepper flakes

2 tablespoons dry Marsala

$1/4$ cup grated Parmesan cheese

VEGETABLES

1 zucchini, sliced lengthwise $1/4$ inch thick

1 eggplant, sliced lengthwise $1/4$ inch thick

1 red bell pepper, quartered

1 yellow bell pepper, quartered

8 medium-sized mushrooms

$1/2$ cup olive oil

8 ounces mozzarella cheese

$1/2$ cup chopped basil

$1/2$ tomato, diced

■ Make the pizza dough one day before you use it; it will have a better flavor and crust.

■ To make the pizza dough, mix dry ingredients in a bowl. Form a well in the center and mix in the water. Mix the dough by hand until it forms a ball, then knead to a smooth texture. Put the dough in a bowl and cover with plastic wrap. Refrigerate 24 hours.

■ Take the dough out of the refrigerator 1 hour before using it. Once the dough is at room temperature, dust your work surface with flour. Roll out the dough to make a 15-inch circle.

■ To make the pizza sauce, drain half the juice out of the can of tomatoes and discard. In a small pan over low heat, sauté the garlic in 1 tablespoon of the olive oil. Add the tomatoes and remaining juice and simmer for a few minutes.

■ In another pan over low heat, combine 3 tablespoons of olive oil, the anchovies, and red pepper flakes. Add the tomato mixture and Marsala and simmer 1 minute. Remove from heat and add the Parmesan.

■ To make the grilled vegetables, brush the vegetables with olive oil and cook on a hot grill for 3 to 5 minutes, or until done. Remove and set aside.

■ Grill the pizza dough over medium heat, rotating the dough so that it does not burn in any area. Turn the dough over and finish the other side. Give each side about 5 minutes or until the dough cracks.

■ Top the cooked crust with the tomato sauce, then layer on the grilled vegetables. Top with shredded mozzarella. Put pizza under the broiler until cheese melts and starts to brown. Remove pizza from oven and top with fresh basil and diced tomato. Cut into slices and serve.

Serves 6 to 8

Cinnamon Rolls

DOUGH

3/4 cup milk

1/4 cup warm water

1/4 cup butter, softened

1/4 cup sugar

2 eggs

1/2 teaspoon salt

2 packages dry active yeast

2 cups bread flour

1 cup whole-wheat flour

SUGAR MIXTURE

1 1/2 cups sweet butter

1/3 cup firmly packed brown sugar

1/3 cup "raw," unrefined sugar

2 tablespoons ground cinnamon

WHITE ICING

2 cups powdered sugar

1/3 cup warm water

Juice of 1/2 orange

■ To make the dough, combine all ingredients in a bowl and knead by hand for about 5 minutes. Form a ball and let it rise for 30 minutes. Roll out the dough to form an 8 x 12-inch rectangle.

■ To make the sugar mixture, melt the butter. Mix the sugars and cinnamon in a bowl. Spread the melted butter over the rolled-out dough, then spread the sugar mixture over the dough. Roll dough into a tube, pinching the seam to seal the roll shut. With the seam side down, cut the log into 1-inch pieces and lay out on a well-greased baking sheet. Space the rolls evenly apart and press each one to flatten slightly. Let the rolls rise until they have doubled in size. Preheat the oven to 350° and bake the rolls for 20 minutes until golden brown. Let them cool for 10 minutes.

■ To make the icing, combine ingredients and mix to smooth. Spread over cinnamon rolls.

Makes 12 rolls

Chocolate Soufflé with Ganache

GANACHE

18 ounces chocolate chips

$^1/_2$ cup evaporated milk

1 cup cream

SOUFFLÉ

3 tablespoons plus $^1/_2$ cup salted butter

$^1/_2$ cup sugar

2 cups milk

$^2/_3$ cup all-purpose flour

5 eggs

$^1/_2$ cup cocoa powder

2 tablespoons Kahlúa

■ To make the ganache, melt the chocolate chips with the evaporated milk and cream in the top of a double boiler, stirring until smooth. Put the mixture in a bowl to cool, then refrigerate.

■ To make the soufflé, butter the sides and bottom of a 2-quart soufflé bowl with the 3 tablespoons of butter. Then add $^1/_2$ cup of sugar, tilting the bowl to evenly coat the inside (sides and bottom) with the sugar. Shake out and discard any excess sugar. Put 2 rounded tablespoons of ganache in the bottom of the bowl and refrigerate.

■ Preheat the oven to 400°.

■ Combine milk and $^1/_2$ cup of the butter in a saucepan and bring to a boil. Add the flour and stir briskly. Remove from the heat when the mixture becomes hard to stir with one hand and pulls away from the sides of the pan.

■ Separate the eggs, saving the whites in a bowl. Stir egg yolks into flour and butter mixture. Add cocoa powder and mix well. Add $^1/_4$ cup of the sugar and the Kahlúa, stirring the mixture until incorporated.

■ In another bowl, whip the egg whites to soft peaks. Add the remaining $^1/_4$ cup of sugar slowly and whip until egg whites are stiff. Fold egg whites into chocolate in three parts. Fill the soufflé bowl and bake at 400° for 25 minutes.

Macadamia Nut Pie

CRUST

$^2/_3$ cup sweet butter

$^2/_3$ cup shortening

3 cups all-purpose flour

1 tablespoon salt

$^1/_2$ cup ice water

Juice of $^1/_2$ lemon

FILLING

5 eggs

1 cup firmly packed brown sugar

2 tablespoons vanilla extract

$^2/_3$ cup light Karo syrup

$^1/_2$ cup sweet butter, melted

$1^1/_2$ cups diced macadamia nuts

$1^1/_2$ cups whole macadamia nuts

■ Preheat oven to 350°.

■ To make the pie crust, cut butter and shortening into the flour until mealy. Add salt, water, and lemon juice, mixing by hand just until incorporated. Refrigerate for 1 hour. Divide dough in half. Roll out one piece of dough into a circle big enough to cover the bottom and sides of a 10-inch-diameter, $2^1/_2$-inch-deep pie pan. Line the pan with the dough and crimp the edges. (Note: This recipe makes enough for two pie crusts, although you will only need one. The extra crust may be shaped into a disc, covered in plastic wrap, and refrigerated for several days.)

■ To make the filling, beat eggs lightly in a bowl. In another bowl, mix the sugar, vanilla, and Karo syrup, then add the melted butter and eggs. Fill the unbaked pie crust with macadamia nuts. Pour sugar-and-egg mixture over nuts. Bake pie for 40 to 45 minutes. Let cool for 15 minutes and serve warm with ice cream.

Makes one 10-inch pie

Fresh Peach and Cardamom Pie

CRUST

$^2/_3$ cup sweet butter

$^2/_3$ cup shortening

3 cups all-purpose flour

1 tablespoon salt

$^1/_2$ cup ice water

Juice of $^1/_2$ lemon

FILLING

1 cup sugar

$^1/_4$ cup cornstarch

1 tablespoon ground cardamom

1 teaspoon ground cinnamon

6 ripe unskinned peaches, sliced

1 cup water

Juice of 1 lime

Zest of 1 lime, minced

1 egg white, beaten lightly

2 teaspoons sugar

PIE CRUST

3 cups all-purpose flour

$^2/_3$ cup sweet butter

$^2/_3$ cup shortening

1 tablespoon salt

$^1/_2$ cup ice water

Juice of $^1/_2$ lemon

■ To make the pie crust, cut butter and shortening into the flour until mealy. Add salt, water, and lemon juice, mixing by hand just until incorporated. Refrigerate for 1 hour. Divide dough into two pieces, one slightly larger than the other. Roll out one piece of dough into a circle big enough to cover the bottom and sides of a 10-inch-diameter, $2^1/_2$-inch-deep pie pan. Line the pan with the dough. Roll out the remaining piece of dough into a circle big enough to easily cover the pie filling and still have extra dough to crimp around the rim of the pie pan.

■ To make the filling, mix the sugar with the cornstarch in a bowl. Stir in the cardamom and cinnamon. Add the peaches and toss to coat evenly. In a small bowl, combine the water, lime juice, and zest. Add to the peaches and toss again. Pour this mixture into the pie shell and top with the other piece of dough. Brush the pie with the beaten egg white and top with 2 teaspoons sugar. Bake in a preheated 350° oven for 1 hour and 15 minutes. Let cool. Cut and serve with vanilla ice cream.

Makes one 10-inch pie

Coconut Haupia Cream Pie

COOKIE CRUST

1 cup unsalted butter

2 teaspoons vanilla

1 egg

2^1/$_2$ cups all-purpose flour

^{1}/$_2$ teaspoon salt

^{1}/$_4$ cup melted unsalted butter

HAUPIA PUDDING

6 ounces coconut milk

^{1}/$_2$ cup sugar

1 cup milk

^{1}/$_4$ cup cornstarch

COCONUT BAVARIAN CREAM

1 rounded tablespoon unflavored gelatin

3 tablespoons water

1^1/$_2$ cups whipping cream

1^1/$_2$ cups milk

6 egg yolks

^{1}/$_2$ cup sugar

^{1}/$_2$ cup shredded sweetened coconut, toasted

- Preheat oven to 350°.

- To make the cookie crust, mix butter and vanilla and cream together. Add the egg, flour, and salt and mix together. Place dough on a greased baking sheet and bake for 15 to 20 minutes. Remove from oven and let cool; refrigerate 1 hour.

- Crumble 2 cups of cookie crust, add melted butter, and mix by hand until blended. When the cookie mixture holds together, it is ready. Press half of the mixture into the bottom of an 8-inch pie pan, working up the sides of the pan and pressing to compact it. (Note: This recipe makes enough for two pie crusts, although you will only need one. The extra crust may be shaped into a disc, covered in plastic wrap, and refrigerated for several days.) Bake 15 to 20 minutes and let cool.

- In a saucepan, combine coconut milk, sugar and ^{1}/$_2$ cup milk. Bring to a slow boil. In a bowl, mix together the remaining ^{1}/$_2$ cup milk and cornstarch. Mix until there are no lumps, then slowly add to the hot mixture, stirring constantly until thick. Remove from stove and pour into pie crust. Refrigerate until cold and set.

■ To make the Coconut Bavarian Cream, soften the gelatin with water in a bowl and set aside. Whip the cream and reserve. Combine the milk, egg yolks, and sugar in a stainless steel bowl and set over a double boiler. Cook until the mixture coats a spoon and you can run a finger through the mixture on the spoon and see that the line remains. Remove the mixture from the heat and add the set gelatin; mix until blended. Set the hot bowl over an ice bath and stir until it cools and starts to thicken. Fold whipped cream into mixture in two stages, incorporating well. Add the coconut. Fill the pie with the cream mixture and smooth over. Refrigerate for 2 hours before serving.

Makes one 8-inch pie

Strawberry-Carrot Cake

CAKE

2 cups sugar

$1/2$ cup vegetable oil

2 eggs

2 cups all-purpose flour

1 teaspoon salt

1 teaspoon baking soda

$1/4$ teaspoon baking powder

2 cups grated carrots

CREAM CHEESE ICING

4 cups powdered sugar

$1/4$ cup hot water

$1/4$ cup sweet butter, at room temperature

$1/4$ cup shortening

1 pound cream cheese

2 pints strawberries, thinly sliced

■ Preheat oven to 350°.

■ To make the cake, mix the sugar, oil, and eggs together. Add the flour, salt, baking soda, baking powder, and carrots. Mix until just incorporated with no lumps. Grease a 10-inch cake pan and fill with batter. Bake for 45 to 50 minutes until firm. Let cool, unmold from pan, and refrigerate.

■ To make the icing, put the powdered sugar in a bowl and add hot water slowly, mixing until smooth. Mix in the butter, then add the shortening and blend. Add the icing to the cream cheese in three stages, scraping the bowl to keep the mixture smooth.

■ Cut the cake into three layers. Ice each of the bottom two layers with $1/4$ inch of cream cheese icing and top with 6 sliced strawberries. Assemble the two layers and add the top layer. Ice the entire cake with cream cheese icing, starting with the top and then the sides. Top the cake with sliced strawberries.

Espresso Torte

8 ounces bittersweet chocolate

4 ounces semisweet chocolate

1 cup sweet butter

$^1/_2$ cup instant freeze-dried coffee

$^1/_2$ cup hot water

5 eggs

1 cup sugar

$^1/_2$ cup corn syrup

1 pint heavy whipping cream

■ In the top of a double boiler, melt the chocolate and butter until the chocolate is completely smooth.

■ Dissolve the instant coffee in the hot water and stir into the melted chocolate. Lightly beat the eggs in a bowl. Add the sugar and corn syrup to the chocolate, then add the eggs to the chocolate mixture. Mix ingredients well.

■ Preheat oven to 350°. Cover the bottom of a 9-inch cake pan with a layer of wax paper or parchment paper. Pour the batter into the pan. Set the cake pan in a water bath and bake for 45 minutes, or until firm in the center. Let the cake cool and gently remove from the pan.

■ When you are ready to serve the cake, beat the whipping cream in a glass bowl with a whisk or electric beater until soft peaks form. Add sugar to taste. Top each piece of cake with whipped cream.

Chocolate-Raspberry Truffle Cake

CHOCOLATE CAKE

$1/2$ cup cocoa powder

$1/2$ cup hot water

2 tablespoons unsalted butter, at room
temperature

2 tablespoons shortening

1 cup sugar

1 cup all-purpose flour

1 teaspoon baking soda

$1/2$ teaspoon salt

4 eggs

$1/2$ cup sour cream

CHOCOLATE TRUFFLE ICING

6 cups powdered sugar

1 cup cocoa powder

$1/2$ cup warm milk

1 cup unsalted butter, at room
temperature

1 tablespoon vanilla extract

GANACHE

18 ounces chocolate chips

$1/2$ cup evaporated milk

1 cup cream

$1^1/2$ cups Chambord

40 raspberries, plus additional for garnish

■ Grease a 9-inch cake pan. Preheat the oven to 350°.

■ To make the chocolate cake, combine the cocoa, $1/4$ cup of the hot water, the butter, and shortening and cream together. Add the sugar, flour, baking soda, and salt; cream together and then scrape down the sides of the bowl. Add remaining hot water, eggs, and sour cream and mix until smooth, about 3 minutes. Pour the batter into the greased pan and bake for 30 minutes, or until firm in the center. Cool on a wire rack, then refrigerate.

■ To make the icing, combine powdered sugar, cocoa, and warm milk in a bowl. (The milk should not be hot, but just warmed to about 100°.) Add butter and vanilla and mix until there are no lumps and the icing is smooth.

■ To make the ganache, melt the chocolate chips, evaporated milk, and cream in the top of a double boiler, stirring until smooth. Remove from heat. Remove the cake from the refrigerator and liberally pour warm ganache over it, covering the entire cake. Smooth over and refrigerate again for at least 1 hour.

▪ Cut the cooled chocolate cake into three layers. Pour $^1/_2$ cup of Chambord over each layer, then add a thin layer of icing to the first layer. Add fresh raspberries to cover. Ice the next layer and cover with raspberries. Add the top layer and ice the whole cake. Garnish as desired with additional raspberries. Refrigerate for 1 hour to set the icing.

▪ NOTE: The ganache can be made ahead of time and refrigerated. When you are ready to use it, warm in a microwave until it is an easily pourable consistency.

Chocolate Zuppa

CHOCOLATE CAKE

$1/2$ cup cocoa powder

$1/2$ cup hot water

2 tablespoons unsalted butter, at room
    temperature

2 tablespoons shortening

1 cup sugar

1 cup all-purpose flour

1 teaspoon baking soda

$1/2$ teaspoon salt

4 eggs

$1/2$ cup sour cream

PASTRY CREAM

2 cups milk

$1/2$ cup sugar

2 tablespoons cornstarch

2 tablespoons all-purpose flour

6 egg yolks

1 teaspoon vanilla extract

1 tablespoon unsalted butter

ZUPPA TOPPING

$1/2$ cup sliced almonds

$1/3$ cup milk

$1/2$ cup hot coffee

$1 1/2$ cups chocolate chips

6 ounces miniature marshmallows

2 tablespoons instant freeze-dried coffee

1 cup Amaretto

- Grease a 9-inch cake pan. Preheat the oven to 350°.

- To make the chocolate cake, combine cocoa, $1/4$ cup of the hot water, butter, and shortening and cream together. Add the sugar, flour, baking soda, and salt; cream together and then scrape down the sides of the bowl. Add remaining hot water, the eggs, and the sour cream and mix until smooth, about 3 minutes. Pour batter into the greased pan and bake for 30 minutes, or until firm. Cool and refrigerate.

- To make the pastry cream, heat the milk until it comes to a boil. In a bowl combine the sugar, cornstarch, and flour. Make a well in the center, add the egg yolks, and slowly stir in the dry ingredients to keep the mixture wet. When the mixture is smooth, pour in half of the hot milk and mix. Then pour the mixture into the pot with the rest of the hot milk and continue to cook until it thickens. Remove from heat. Add vanilla and butter and mix. Cover with plastic wrap and let cool.

- Toast the almonds in a 350° oven for 10 minutes until brown.

Chocolate Zuppa continued

▦ In the top of a double boiler, heat the milk, hot coffee, chocolate chips, marshmallows, and instant coffee until the chocolate and marshmallows are melted and the mixture is smooth. Remove from heat.

▦ Cut the chocolate cake in half to make two layers. Place the top layer in the bottom of a glass bowl. Pour $^1/_2$ cup of Amaretto over the layer, using a pastry brush to distribute evenly. Add enough Zuppa topping to cover the bottom layer. Cover pastry cream in a smooth layer, then place the other layer of cake on top and pour the remaining Amaretto over the top. Add another layer of Zuppa topping. Refrigerate at least 1 hour. Top with toasted almonds and serve.

Chocolate Truffles

GANACHE

18 ounces chocolate chips

$^1/_2$ cup evaporated milk

1 cup cream

$^1/_2$ cup cocoa powder, or almonds, macadamia nuts, or hazelnuts, finely chopped

▦ To make the ganache, melt the chocolate chips with the evaporated milk and cream in the top of a double boiler, stirring until smooth. Remove from heat. Put the ganache in the refrigerator to cool, about 1 hour, and chill a large baking sheet. When the ganache is cool, remove from the refrigerator. Using a truffle scooper, scoop out a small ball, then roll it in cocoa or nuts and set on the cold baking sheet. Repeat until all the chocolate has been used.

Makes 10 to 12 truffles

Lychee Sorbet

4 (20-ounce) cans lychees in light syrup

1$\frac{1}{2}$ cups sugar

1 mango, peeled and diced

6 to 8 strawberries, stemmed and diced

3 to 4 sections honeydew melon, diced

■ Drain the fruit, reserving the juice in a bowl. In a saucepan over high heat, combine 4 cups of the lychee juice with the sugar and bring to a boil. Remove from heat and set aside. Purée lychee fruit in a blender or food processor and strain the fruit into the sugar syrup. Freeze the mixture in a gelato or ice cream maker following the manufacturer's instructions.

■ Combine the mango, strawberries, and melon. Scoop the sorbet into serving dishes and garnish with the diced fruit.

Makes 1 quart

NOTES FROM BOB

One of the passions that I've had for several years is to write a book on food in the fashion of M.F.K. Fisher's *Serve It Forth*. When I was very young someone gave me a copy of her celebrated book and it excited me in many ways. Even though it had just a few recipes, I felt it was one of the greatest books ever written about food.

Since that time I have seen very few books of that quality. Most books on food are pure cookbooks. This book has many recipes, but it is also a journal about food, which is why I have included many recollections of some of the great gastronomical moments I've experienced as well as some great examples of serendipity. (As you know, serendipity is the unexpected occurrence of a pleasurable or important event.)

■ ■ ■

I remember being very little and sitting around the large table in the kitchen of our fabulous house in Glens Falls, New York. Even though we had a formal dining room, we ate most of our meals in the kitchen. I can see Grandma Marie making her delicious gnocchi and risotto as I sat eagerly at the table, waiting for her to complete the meal so I could have my first bite.

■ ■ ■

The best minestrone I ever tasted is linked in my memory with a classic football game. In 1943, when I was ten years old, my Dad began taking my brother, my mother, and me to New York City to watch the annual Notre Dame–Army game. Notre Dame had been a perennial football power before the war but since the war started Army had recruited all the great players. Army had two of the greatest backs in the history of football, Glen Davis and Doc Blanchard. In 1943, Notre Dame got walloped 48 to 0. In 1944, Army made it even worse and beat them 59 to 0. In 1945 the war was over, and Notre Dame had gotten back many of their great players. Going into the last period, the score was 0 to 0 when all of a sudden Army's Doc Blanchard, a bull of a man with fantastic speed, broke through the line and was running for a touchdown. Out of nowhere came a player who made one of the greatest shoestring tackles in the history of football. The player was Johnny Lujack, who was Notre Dame's quarterback. This will probably never happen again because nowadays quarterbacks do not play defense. After the game my father and mother took us to their favorite New York restaurant, Zucca's, which no longer exists. Zucca's had the greatest minestrone soup that I have ever had. It was very thick, had beans in it, and an unbelievable taste. I've never had a minestrone that could even compare to it. By the way, the game ended 0 to 0.

■ ■ ■

Henri Soulé was the proprietor of the famous Le Pavillon restaurant in New York, which most people in the 1960s considered the finest restaurant in America. I met him at the racetrack one afternoon. Neither Henri nor I was very much interested in racing, so we spent four hours talking about food and discussing all the wonderful things that have to do with the culinary life. It was one of the most memorable days of my life—and was another inspiration for me to become a restauranteur.

■ ■ ■

My wife Gail and I had a fabulous lunch at Roger Verge's Moulin de Mougins in Mougins, France, in 1983. The restaurant was beautiful, the service was impeccable, and the people who worked there were joyous and extremely friendly. Our maître d' was from the same town in Alsace-Lorraine as my grandmother and gave us service beyond the norm. When we walked into the restaurant, he immediately escorted us to the best table in the house.

■ ■ ■

The first time I drank Dom Perignon was in 1966. Dave Abramson and his wife Sally came to our house for dinner and brought a bottle of Dom Perignon to accompany the fresh beluga caviar that I provided. It was the first time I had eaten fresh caviar, and it was also the first time I had Dom Perignon. It was a terrific taste experience. Since that time both Dave and I have been trying to match the taste of that first Dom Perignon. For thirty years we haven't been able to achieve it, but the memory lingers on.

■ ■ ■

I would have to rank a meal I had at Luchows restaurant in Manhattan among the five best dinners of my life.

In 1961 I had just finished Massachusetts Mutual's annual "quota buster" contest, which consisted of six weeks of high-intensity selling. I had done extremely well, leading my agency in total production. Harry Copeland, my mentor, invited the top producers to have dinner with him at Luchows on 14th Street. At the time, it was the premiere German restaurant in America. Even though it had the oom-pa-pa music and was extemely large, it was still able to exude a stately air of elegance.

The meal started with fresh Cape Cod oysters. These are oysters that are transported to Cape Cod, where they grow to their enormous size. The cold waters of the North Atlantic give these gigantic bivalves a unique quality. Next came filet of venison with an unbelievable Cumberland Sauce. The venison was tender and juicy and the sauce complemented it perfectly. The maitre d' concluded the meal with one of the most spectacular desserts one can imagine. He called it a *Pfannküchen*. This is a large pancake (the size of a medium pizza) cooked in a brazier at tableside. The pancake rises two inches, has apples and other fruit inside it, and is served with a sauce similar to that on a crêpe suzette.

■ ■ ■

On the first night after I moved to New York City to work for Harry Copeland in his insurance agency, he invited Sally and me to Chambord, which was his (and many New Yorkers') favorite elegant restaurant. Even though I had been to many fine restaurants, I was very excited, for this had been described as the ultimate bastion of French cuisine. Unfortunately, against Harry's advice, I ordered pheasant under glass, which I had read about for years in my copious studies of gastronomy. It seemed to me that I could not achieve culinary maturity if I did not experience this celebrated combination. It was one of the biggest disappointments of my life—unbearably dry and stringy. I have never ordered it since, nor will I order it again. Fortunately the *pommes soufflés* were fantastic and everything else I had with the meal was terrific.

■ ■ ■

For our third anniversary, I decided to take Sally to the most expensive restaurant in Washington, D.C. The Rive Gauche was a very elegant French restaurant, with a maître d', captains, sommeliers, and all of the accouterments one would expect. We had a complete meal and a bottle of wine. How much do you think that meal cost? The answer is $17, including tip. Hard to believe, but true. Of course, it seemed like a lot at the time. I remember going back the next day to my army buddies and asking them incredulously, "Do you know how much money I spent on dinner last night? Seventeen dollars!" Today that won't even buy you two cups of coffee in Tokyo.

■ ■ ■

The Palm restaurant had opened its first branch in Washington, D.C., and I was one of their best customers. I even had a special table. The highlight of my children's birthdays each year was dinner at the Palm. We would order gigantic steaks and lobsters, their fabulous potatoes, their great salads, and their terrific cheesecake and have a feast that would fill us for days.

One night one of my friends told me he was entertaining very important clients and wanted to impress them as much as he possibly could. I told him he should go to the Palm. I called up ahead of time and told the manager that my friend wanted the biggest lobster they could possibly find to be served to his group. As they we were finishing their appetizers, a 14-pound lobster on a leash walked across the dining room and presented itself!

■ ■ ■

The Gritti Palace is a little gem of a hotel on the Grand Canal in Venice. I arrived to discover that the bar was called Bar Longhi and that the manager's mother was a Longhi. Needless to say, I feel at home in this great hotel.

■ ■ ■

Watching one of the most beautiful sunsets I've ever seen in the northern Italian district of Piedmont, then going to dinner at the famous restaurant da Guido, is another favorite memory. We sat down for a meal that consisted of a truffle salad, truffle soup, truffle pasta, and the meal finally ended with a main course of guinea hen smothered with truffles. (Unfortunately, my wife Gail did not like white truffles, as their smell is extremely pungent.) The only thing missing was truffle sorbet! We had a marvelous time talking to Guido in his wine cellar for an hour before dinner, but the total experience was marred by trufflitis.

■ ■ ■

I used to love having lunch during the 1960s at a little Manhattan restaurant called Maria's. She had the greatest fettuccine I've ever eaten. One day I walked into Maria's restaurant and ordered the fettuccine. When the meal was over, I said, "Maria, there's something different about the fettuccine noodles." She said, "You know, Mr. Longhi you are the only one who noticed it. We had to change our noodle maker for two weeks because my regular noodle maker has been sick." Then she looked at me and smiled, "You know your noodles."

■ ■ ■

In Manhattan during the '60s, there was an expensive and elegant restaurant next to my office called Giambelli. Frank Giambelli was a super restaurateur from Milano. In those days we would have a three-course lunch that consisted of an appetizer, main course, and dessert, and the bill was about $7.

Four or five years later I took a group of clients to lunch at Giambelli. When we walked in I noticed a sign that said "tartufi bianci flown in from Italy." This was in October when the white truffles are at their peak. I tried to convince everyone to order the truffles, and fortunately only one person agreed. We ordered two plates of fettuccine with truffles. The bill came and I was shocked beyond belief. They charged me $44 for each pasta dish. (In those days $44 was like $500 today.) The ironic part of this story is that this was the first time I had picked up the tab as all the previous meals had been hosted by my clients.

▦ ▦ ▦

I spent wonderful nights, weeks, and months at the Huntington Hotel in San Francisco enjoying the room service created by the fabulous chef Gloria Ciccarone Nehls. Gloria has been at the Huntington for the past 17 years. All of the food that she creates is wonderful, and no one makes better soup.

▦ ▦ ▦

Gail and I once went to the gigantic restaurant Jumbo in the harbor of Hong Kong with our friends Bob and Jenny Theleen. Jenny is Chinese and a great gourmet. She and I ordered and ate so much food that the waiters smiled constantly and gave us unbelievable service. According to Jenny it was the best meal she ever had at this restaurant, which had a reputation of catering to foreign tourists. One thing I have learned is if you want to get the best possible service and food at a Chinese restaurant, order lots of expensive food, eat with gusto, and leave a big tip. You can go back to the same restaurant five years later and they not only will remember you, they will make sure you enjoy a wonderful feast.

▦ ▦ ▦

After raising hell all night when I was in my teens, I would go to a little restaurant in South Glens Falls called Massie's and at 2 A.M. order spaghetti with marinara sauce, accompanied by a Coca-Cola. I don't drink Coke very often now days but when I have spaghetti made by southern Italians from the northeastern United States, I must confess, it's my favorite beverage.

▦ ▦ ▦

In 1939, when I was living in Torrington, Connecticut, and only six years old, somebody brought our family a brand new dish they had purchased in New Haven. It was a round piece of bread with tomatoes and cheese on it, and they called it a pizza. There are many theories as to when pizza started in America. One of the stories that is most subscribed to is that the first pizza was commercially sold in New Haven, Connecticut around 1939. There is, however, another story that pizza was first sold in New York City in 1906. I have no idea of what happened between 1906 and 1939, but it is possible that I may have eaten one of the first commercial pizzas ever sold in America.

■ ■ ■

I once had the pleasure of standing in the largest suite in the stately Peninsula Hotel in Hong Kong, attending a party for all the guests to watch the fabulous fireworks that celebrate the coming of the Chinese New Year. It's one of the greatest displays of pyrotechnics imaginable.

■ ■ ■

One of my fondest memories from 1964 is of becoming a member of Winged Foot County Club, where I would play nine holes of golf on one of America's greatest courses, stop and have a fantastic lunch of the best chicken salad sandwiches imaginable, then go back to the tee and play nine more holes. On Sunday mornings, my colleague and mentor Harry Copeland and I would drive to Winged Foot to play 18 holes, then jump into Harry's car and drive back to Yankee Stadium for the Giant's football game. Harry apparently had a New York City policeman in his employ. The policeman would take our car when we arrived and when the game was over, our car would be ready for us. Valet service à la NYPD. Harry naturally gave the officer a handsome tip. I'll always remember those autumn Sundays. We did this for five years, until our company moved to Washington, D.C. Driving to the first game in Washington, I asked Harry where we would park. He told me not to worry, he would take care of it. We approached a policeman and Harry handed him a twenty-dollar bill, expecting the police to do what had been done in New York. The policeman looked at us and said, "Get the hell out of here" and refused to park Harry's car. The next week Harry moved back to New York City.

■ ■ ■

Rio de Janeiro has a fantastic restaurant, the GrattaMare, where I ate four times a week when I was visiting there. It is run by a gentleman from the La Marche area of Italy who serves all kinds of grilled fish and crustaceans with terrific pastas.

■ ■ ■

In San Francisco, some of my favorite restaurants include the venerable Stars; Lulu's, which has a calamari pizza that is unbelievable; and Little Joe's, run by Frank from Genoa. One of the great things to do is to sit at the counter and order Frank's fantastic squid creation, which he cooks quickly on top of the stove. It's not deep-fried, and it's not like anything you've had before.

The Great Eastern on Jackson Street is one of my favorite Chinese restaurants. When you walk in, you see all the live seafood swimming in tanks. These range from Dungeness crab to abalone to lobster to three or four different kinds of fish and also one thing I've never seen in another restaurant: live frogs. Make sure that you order the fresh prawns steamed and served with a garlic sauce. The bok choy is fantastic, too. Have the Dungeness crab salt-and-pepper style. It's to die for. Another great Cantonese restaurant, the Hong Kong Flower Lounge on Geary Street, has all of the wonderful seafood that Hong Kong is so famous for. They also do a terrific job with Peking duck.

■ ■ ■

Venice, Italy, is one of my favorite places in the world to eat. The Madonna trattoria has the best grilled eel. I would travel thousands of miles just to have this dish. Everything else they serve is the best. Another great restaurant is La Corte Sconta, again specializing in the great seafood, risotto and pastas which are indigenous to this terrific gourmet paradise. Harry's Bar is an experience you may want to try when you visit Venice for the first time the food is great, but the prices are extremely high.

■ ■ ■

I have not dined in Washington, D.C., for years but one of the best places to eat is a very small restaurant called the Calvert Cafe, run by a Jordanian woman referred to as Mama. In my recollection she still has the best babaganoush I've ever had in my life. It is an eggplant dip eaten with pita bread. When it is done properly it is brilliant.

■ ■ ■

I mentioned earlier the great Hotel Royale in San Remo, Italy, where Ivan is a fantastic concierge. There are several great pizzerias in San Remo, among them Pizzeria 64, Maria Blue, and Italia.

■ ■ ■

Lake Como is definitely one of the most beautiful lakes in the world. (I was brought up in Glens Fall, New York, nine miles from Lake George, which is referred to as the Lake Como of America.) The most famous hotel on Lake Como, and maybe in the world, is Villa d'Este, situated the west side of the lake. The Villa d'Este is definitely beautiful but I found the cuisine sadly lacking. A hotel I found much more charming, with great food and a beautiful location, is the Villa Serbelloni, which is on the other side of the lake in a little village called Bellagio. I especially remember awakening my first morning there and smelling the fantastically fragrant flowers. It was a smell that haunted me for years and every time I get near anything that is redolent of this smell I am immediately taken back to the wonderful time I spent at the Serbellone. Our room had fourteen-foot ceilings with frescoes in the style of Michaelangelo.

■ ■ ■

Sitting with 26,000 people in the open air of the opera house in Verona, which was the provincial capitol of the Roman empire and where I saw the great opera Carmen, was once-in-a-lifetime experience.

■ ■ ■

Restaurant San Francisco in Montecatini Terme, is run by my very dear friends Paulo and Louisa Michelotti. Paulo is a wizard at cooking, serving, hosting, and everything else it takes to make a great restaurant. His food is terrific, his attitude is wonderful, and his wife, Louisa, is also a beautiful person.

■ ■ ■

The little town of Forte des Marmi is on the Mediterranean less than one hundred miles from Florence. This is one of the world's most elegant towns. At night, the townspeople, regardless of their age, ride around on bicycles, mingle in the town center, talk, eat pizza, and generally have fun. I was so impressed with this town that one of my goals is to go there, rent a villa, and spend a month or two just enjoying the terrific atmosphere.

■ ■ ■

One of the most serene towns in Italy, and a place that inspired me to write, is Assisi, the home of Saint Francis. There is a hotel called Subasio that I recommend. If you stay there, ask for room 25, which has a balcony overlooking a fantastic verdant valley that goes on for miles. It is one of the few places you can watch a horizon sunrise and a horizon sunset. What I remember the most is standing on the balcony at sunset when all of a sudden thousands of birds appeared. These birds flew right to me and around me, and became part of my existence. I have never experienced such closeness to flying birds any other place that I have ever been.

■ ■ ■

The area surrounding Rimini, on the Adriatic coast, has unbelievable seafood. One of my favorite things is a crustacean resembling shrimp, called cannocchi. Cannocchi is so delicate that it can only be experienced on the Adriatic, because it cannot be frozen.

■ ■ ■

In 1984, Gail and I stayed at a small hotel in Ravello called Palumbo. Ravello is located 1,100 feet above the Tyrrhenian Sea on the Amalfi coast in southern Italy. The patron of the hotel, Pasquale Vuilleumier, was an eighty-five-year-old man who was extremely charming and had a wine cellar that was unbelievable. On Gail's birthday he presented her with wine bottled in the year of her birth. It was a fantastic bottle of wine, coupled with a meal that was great. It was one of the few hotels where I've enjoyed eating the food. In most cases I eschew eating in hotel restaurants.

■ ■ ■

The owner of a very small restaurant on the Island of Capri, called La Cisterna, would sauté whole fish in hot olive oil in a cast-iron pan for a few minutes. He would then put the pan into his 600° pizza oven to finish cooking. The results were spectacular.

■ ■ ■

During a week in Sicily we stayed at a terrific hotel in Palermo, the Villa Agea. Driving around the island, we eventually ended up in one of the most elegant and beautiful towns imaginable, Taormina.

NOTES FROM A CHAIR MAN

Many restauranteurs find a great location to build their restaurant. They spend two to four million dollars on a beautiful physical plant, hire a top-notch chef, buy only the best products, and forget one thing. They spend about twenty-seven cents on their chairs.

Chairs are one of the most important things in a restaurant. A diner is going to sit from one to three hours, and their meal will be either enhanced or diminished depending on the state of their posterior. If you are uncomfortable, your dining experience is diminished. If you are comfortable and feel good about the way you're sitting, you are going to be a happy diner.

When I opened Longhi's, I was very fortunate to find ninety antique chairs that had come from a hotel in Tacoma, Washington. I spent 5 dollars apiece for these chairs, and another 20 dollars each to restore them. In the last twenty years I have invested more than one hundred thousand dollars to have these chairs reproduced. (It is interesting to note that sixty or seventy of the ninety original chairs I bought are still in use, whereas more than half of the five hundred reproductions have had to be replaced.) It's been a large expense but, in my opinion, a very worthwhile one. My advice to anyone who wants to go into the restaurant business is to make sure you have chairs that are very comfortable—the type of chair that makes eating a pleasure instead of a task.

I recently noted that a restauranteur who is a great chef and had fantastic food and a fairly beautiful restaurant went out of business. My problem with that restaurant was that the chairs were so uncomfortable that my meal was tarnished to such a degree that I decided never to go there again. I'm sure that if this restauranteur had put as much thought into the chairs as she had put into the rest of the restaurant, it would still be in business.

PUTTING THE SQUEEZE ON BOTTLED O.J.

Before I opened Longhi's, one of the things I most enjoyed at home each morning was freshly squeezed orange juice. When I went traveling I would always ask the waiter if the orange juice was fresh, and they would invariably say, "Yes, it is." And I would say, "Do you take a little round orange thing, cut it and then squeeze it?" They would reply, "No, we don't squeeze it here, sir." So obviously it wasn't fresh. Fresh means that you are served the orange juice minutes after the squeezing process takes place.

When I opened Longhi's, one of the first things I insisted on was that we had fresh orange juice—and I meant fresh in the true sense, not as it has come to be understood in America. I now believe that many people think "fresh" means that at one time during its existence the juice was indeed fresh, even though that may have been three years ago.

Another funny thing happened when my wife Gail and I were returning from a trip to Brazil. We stopped in southern Florida, in the fashionable town of Key West, and we walked into a pizzeria. Gail asked for a pizza with mushrooms. She asked the pizza maker, who was a boy in his teens, "Are the mushrooms fresh?" He replied emphatically, "Yes, they are—I guarantee it." So she ordered the mushroom pizza. A few minutes later the pizza arrived, topped with what were obviously canned mushrooms. She then said to the young man, "These mushrooms are not fresh!" To which the boy replied, "Yes, they are—I opened that can five minutes ago!" He was not joking. (Another phrase that is irritating to me is "fresh frozen." What's my other choice—frozen rotten?)

WHAT NEXT: NO PLATES?

I've noticed over the past few years that many restaurants no longer have spoons on the table. My suspicion is that someone wrote an article in one of the trade journals stating that a restaurant could save money leaving the spoon out of the place setting. (It is true that spoons seem to be the one thing above all others that disappears from a restaurant.) This practice has become so rife that in more than half of the restaurants I frequent there are no spoons on the table. If this is a method of saving money, I hope no one writes an article extolling the virtues of not having forks and knives, because obviously that would really save lots of money.

POPPY MORGAN, a truly wonderful human being and a dear friend, died while I was writing this book. His presence in my life was extremely beneficial. When we opened Longhi's, he volunteered to help us get started, even though he had three large restaurants of his own to run in California. My daughter Gabrielle, who at that time was running the kitchen, said that we never could have done it without Poppy. This book was partly inspired by Poppy. When I went to Europe thirteen years ago, he gave me a writing tablet and encouraged me to do some writing while traveling.

For the past two years, Poppy and I hosted a cooking show, which was extremely enjoyable and very helpful to Longhi's. Poppy made the arrangements for the initial show, which got me started on my television career.

When I think about Poppy, one particular anecdote from his first restaurant in Palm Springs comes to mind. As he told the story, one day a couple of guys walked in who looked like they were in the mob. They said, "We're going to bring in forty people tonight and we want you to make us a feast!" In his ever-positive way, Poppy said, "Sure I can make you a feast." Not knowing what he was going to do, he walked into the back room and saw two doors sitting on the floor. A great idea popped into his mind: why not cover the doors with tablecloths and load them up with ribs, chicken, various vegetables, steak, and whatever else was in the kitchen panty. That night, two waiters picked up the doors piled with food and carried them to the dining room while Poppy announced, "Gentlemen, here's your feast." The guys went nuts. From that moment forward, Poppy became very famous for his feasts.

In the late '70s, you could go to any one of Poppy's exciting restaurants, called the Great American Food and Beverage Company, in Los Angeles and have someone like Robin Williams, Katie Segal, or Rickie Lee Jones wait on you. When they were finished, they would sing a song or tell a joke. One of the things that made those restaurants famous were the feasts he had created on the spur of the moment back in Palm Springs.

Thanks, Poppy, for being you.

INDEX